The Freedom to Recover

An evolutionary and realistic guide to overcoming alcoholism without the dogma of the AA church and its 12 step religion

"You are NOT Powerless"

Rolf Ankermann

Intuitive Action LLC
Bayville, NY

Cover Design by Tugboat Design
Editor, Jill Wendrow
Bio Photo Credit, Jill Wendrow

Intuitive Action LLC, Bayville, NY 11709

www.thefreedomtorecover.com

ISBN 978-0-9887964-2-3 (Paperback edition)
ISBN 978-0-9887964-0-9 (Kindle edition)
ISBN 978-0-9887964-1-6 (ePub edition)

Altruistic and empathetic intent,
followed by intuitive and thoughtful action,
equals an authentic and meaningful life.

~

Rolf Ankermann
2013

Contents

Introduction

The freedom to recover does not offer a "program" for sobriety but rather, suggests a complete reversal of how alcohol addiction should be both viewed and addressed.

For far too long, alcoholism has been seen as a "disease" in which those afflicted have absolutely no personal control over their plight. This concept has been both accepted and forwarded by healthcare professionals, the media, the psychiatric community, rehabilitation specialists, the courts and society as a whole. By far the largest proponent of this stance is taken by the organization of Alcoholics Anonymous (AA), which emphatically states that those suffering from alcoholism are powerless over their addiction unless they surrender their will and turn their lives over to a "higher power".

I propose, as do scores of others that have independently beaten their addictions, that the individual is not "powerless", but rather, that they in fact have the freedom to turn their lives around.

Some people would argue that to take such a stand of individual empowerment would be anti-religious or anti-spiritual. I would argue the exact opposite. I believe that mankind's greatest gift is that of free-will, the ability and responsibility to make sound choices. For it is only through this "power" that we can choose to do the right thing and thus be in harmony with ourselves and the universe, or God if you will.

The success rate for those that attempt recovery through AA, or any other form of treatment for that matter, is widely debated. Some people put that number at around 5%, while the "professionals" obviously claim a vastly higher competence in achieving lasting sobriety. Whatever the actual number is, I believe that a new paradigm is long overdue.

This book is divided into two parts. Being that Alcoholics Anonymous is almost universally accepted as "the answer" for those suffering the effects of alcoholism, the first part takes a long and necessary hard look at AA's program of recovery and brings into question the very core of its philosophy, debatable logic and religious leanings.

AA's two part lie of powerlessness and surrender sends the wrong message. That message is that the best that one can hope for is to become a "recovering" alcoholic who maintains his or her sobriety through their religiously based 12 step program.

Can you live a sober life as a member of AA? Well yes you can, but its program is merely a bandage in which its members survive "one day at a time" for eternity. The cost, in terms of lost personal freedom and independence, is quite simply, too high.

AA members claim that "one day at a time" living is all about being present and doing what you have to do in order to stay sober just for today. In reality, the AA way demands that you continually relive your sinful past and fear for your future unless you remain a loyal AA sheep and unquestioningly follow their guidance. Existing this way is the complete opposite of living in the moment!

Besides the requirement of surrendering, AA's 12 step path to recovery is all about creating a sin list, confessing said sins and then to find atonement by apologizing and trying to make amends by doing the right thing. That's all fine and dandy but it has NOTHING to do with addiction and trying to overcome it.

While the organization does possess many attributes that are beneficial, particularly during the beginning stages of sobriety, its insistence that a lifelong association as a participating member is necessary in order for one to achieve lasting sobriety has no basis in fact and actually hinders personal growth. Credit will be given to AA's useful traits but the emphasis here must be to debunk the myths that lead so many into living a life in which they depend on AA for their very survival.

A healthier and infinitely more satisfying and empowering way to approach life is to embrace the gift of free will, decide to decide and to chart your own path.

Part two will discuss various methods and ways of thinking that will enable you to give your life meaning and purpose. You will discover that an alcohol and drug free life is not only possible, but enjoyable, rewarding and totally in your "power" to attain.

You will find no cookie cutter program with cozy little steps here. I'm not going to tell you what to do. Borrowing from basic psychology, eastern philosophy, existentialism, life experience, logic and common sense, I will propose ideas that will enable you to re-create your reality and live a life of unlimited potential. I will ask you to question the questions and to find your own answers.

Life is not stagnant and one needs to embrace change in order to grow and evolve.

Hey, if being the master of your own destiny doesn't work for you, there is always AA. But you can and will do it if you want it. You are not powerless and you don't have to turn your life or self-will over to anybody or anything.

Sobriety is a choice and the choice is yours alone. Let the journey begin.

A word of caution

Whether you embrace AA's position of personal powerlessness over alcohol or my idea of embracing acceptance and taking responsibility for one's own life, it is time to take some form of action to alleviate your addictive condition. Again, do NOT attempt to halt your addiction suddenly (Cold Turkey) without consulting a medical doctor first.

At the very least, immediate cessation of alcohol consumption will cause a wide array of discomfort. At its worst, it can be life threatening. While much of what will be discussed in this book will apply to all forms of addiction, I will keep my observations of detoxification and withdrawal to that of alcoholism.

I personally did not consult with a doctor or do any research when I decided to quit and as a result had no idea of what to expect or how to deal with it. The first few days are clearly the worst. I experienced trembling hands to the point that I had to hold a cup of coffee with two hands in order to keep from spilling it all over the place. Sleep was nearly impossible and was accompanied by hot/cold periods to the point where the sheets would be soaking wet from sweat. Along with this was an itchy sensation that was incredibly discomforting. A sense of restlessness is also most likely. I just couldn't sit still and paced around incessantly. Other possible effects of withdrawal that I mercifully did not experience include convulsions and seizures, hallucinations (the DT's), nausea and vomiting and a lack of interest in eating.

It's pretty easy to see why many people at this point give up and grab a bottle to make this all go away! Don't make the same mistake of starting this process ignorant of the hurdles you will face. Learn about what you will be dealing with!

Part One

"The emperor has no clothes"
Exposing AA's myths and the
faulty logic on which they are based

Chapter 1

AA's goals fall short

From the outset I want to make it abundantly clear that it is not the sole intention of this book to harm or degrade the institution of Alcoholics Anonymous, which has clearly over time proven to be an effective and somewhat successful resource for those seeking relief from the pain, misery and enslavement of alcoholism. Rather, like any organization, in order to endure and remain relevant and useful, it must evolve and improve on a continual basis. Unfortunately this is highly unlikely to occur because the entire program of AA is based on the unquestioned ideas and conclusions put forth by its deceased co-founder, Bill Wilson.

One of the most glaring fallacies of the entire AA program is the idea that alcoholism is an incurable disease or "allergy" as it was referred to back in the day. As a result of that premise, AA's loftiest goal is for its members to maintain their sobriety on a daily basis so that they are able to "live" with their disease. The ultimate goal of recovery, however, should be to beat your addiction!

That being said, AA can be extremely effective in early sobriety to combat feelings of isolation and in filling up some of the many hours that were once filled by living in an alcoholic haze.

What AA does well?

AA's team spirit is where I believe participation in its organization is most beneficial. Alcoholics/addicts tend to be very distrustful of the world at large and are reluctant to share their feelings, emotions and fears with anybody. Those barriers, however, do tend to break down when surrounded by other people who have lived through the same ordeal. It's a matter of trust. Therapists and counselors can have all the education in the world and be truly passionate about helping their patients, but unless they've "been there", most addicts feel that they just don't get it. There is comfort in knowing that there are other people just like us who have shared similar experiences. Most alcoholics have slowly but steadily placed themselves into a pattern of isolation and that can only contribute to the escalation of their downward spiral and sense of hopelessness. From an emotional standpoint, it is during the beginning stage of recovery when some form of outside help is essential. Whether you utilize an inpatient rehabilitation facility, an outpatient service, a drug or alcohol counselor, psychiatrist, psychologist or AA, do not, if at all possible, try to do it all alone. Chances are that you will become an emotional rollercoaster and therefore, surrounding yourself with supportive and knowledgeable folks who can "feel your pain" is invaluable!

It is also during the first days, weeks and months of sobriety when one is most susceptible to a relapse. When the going gets tough, which is almost inevitable during these times, a quick fix with your addictive drug is extraordinarily tempting. Just one slip, however, can lead you right back to your addiction/alcoholism as if no attempt at sobriety had ever been initiated.

As previously mentioned, a huge challenge of early sobriety is an excess of new found free time. Think about how many hours of the day alcoholics/addicts spend in planning, acquiring, hiding and using their drug of choice. Idle time can very easily lead one towards boredom, frustration, loneliness and depression. If one does not fill up these blocks of time with constructive and rewarding activities, relapse is an extremely probable outcome. Going to AA meetings at this stage of recovery is a productive way to eat up some of those empty hours.

However, AA's premise that you will forever have to keep alcohol at bay "one day at a time" through participation in its program is a life sentence that is neither healthy nor true! AA's take is that you need to be reminded of your addictive personal history on a daily basis, otherwise, history as the saying goes, is bound to repeat itself. I disagree and feel that one can and should "graduate" from AA and leave their addiction in the past where it belongs. Why would you want to make this sad chapter of your life a daily part of your existence? It makes no sense! Learn from it and move on with your life.

AA's obsession with time

One way in which AA reinforces this idea of eternal day to day sobriety is through its obsession of acknowledging and celebrating its members' length of sobriety. Cute little coins are given for "new or just coming back", 1 month sober, 2 months, 1 year, 4 years, etc. It never ends. Are we children that need to get our gold star for doing a good job? It reminds me of the conversations that inmates in prison have; "How long you in for"? Unlike jail, however, the AA ideal here is for a life sentence for everyone.

This whole idea is further reinforced every time you raise your hand to speak at an Alcoholics Anonymous meeting. The standard way of introducing yourself is to say, "Hi, I'm Rolf and I'm an alcoholic". I'm sorry but if I don't drink any more then do not make me label myself as an alcoholic. It's both demeaning and untrue! If you're obese but lose the weight should I still call you fat? It's the same thing. The whole notion of being a "recovering alcoholic" is just another tool used by the organization to keep you eternally locked into its program. There needs to be a paradigm shift forwarding the concept that addiction can be cured and not simply endured.

AA's antiquated religious basis

I believe that AA has the responsibility to widen its scope so as to both realistically acknowledge and help those that cannot buy into its fundamentally religious foundation.

AA has unfortunately driven away many who may have been helped through its teachings by its reliance with God and AA as the only answers. Yes there is an escape clause for agnostics, atheists and those of a secular nature, but it is clear that even AA's 2nd step; "Came to believe that a Power greater than ourselves could restore us to sanity", is to manifest itself into a belief and reliance in God as is blatantly stated in its 3rd step which states; "Made a decision to turn our will and our lives over to the care of God as we understood Him."

AA's 12 steps are clearly a religion and AA itself, its church. This could not be made any clearer than by the fact that God is featured in at least five of those steps. Organized religion provides to its members purpose, peace and a sense of belonging and community. There is nothing necessarily wrong with this as I believe that for a great number of people suffering with addiction, their underlying cause for having become thus inflicted lies in a longing for some sort of spiritual basis for life which has eluded them. There is, however, a huge difference between following an organized religion and having a sense of spirituality.

The question then becomes how AA is to help those that already have a strong faith and belief along with those that are agnostic and secular. Finding God or a sense of spirituality is wonderful but it is NOT a pre-requisite for beating your addiction!!!!

A few words about Bill

Bill Wilson, AA's co-founder and undisputed leader, found God and that was his miracle cure. He was in the hospital going through the DT's (delirium tremens) while at the same time being treated with the hallucinogenic herb belladonna and a host of barbiturates. It was at this time that Bill claimed to have experienced a God inspired religious conversion. He begged God to show himself and God presumably obliged by appearing as a bright white light. Bill then proceeded to have a vision of being transported to a mountain top where a wind of spirit blew his obsession to drink away.

Gee Bill, I guess in this day and age we can all take a tab of acid and have a Moses epiphany too! Speaking of LSD, Bill did massive experimenting with that after his sobriety and the founding of AA as well-**but he didn't drink!!!!**

For him this was the answer and for a small percentage of people, finding God or a sense of spirituality may very well be the missing piece to helping them overcome their unhappiness and pain. The 12 step religion might actually work for these folks. What about everybody else though? Try implanting Alcoholics Anonymous or a rock in place of the word God in the steps and see how well that works-It doesn't!

Bill was an incredibly compassionate, intuitive and tireless champion of the pursuit of recovery. His intention was truly visionary. Unfortunately, he was also a very sick man with many personal issues and a quick summary here is in order.

Bill suffered from clinical depression with some episodes lasting as long as eleven years.

While he overcame his addiction to alcohol, he was never able to tame his need for copious amounts of caffeine and nicotine. He referred to both as mere commodities and practically advocated their use. Go to any AA meeting and there you will find bottomless pots of coffee and chain smokers communing both before and after the meetings. His chain smoking habit ultimately caused his death.

Mr. Wilson had many adulterous relationships throughout his entire marriage, most notably a long standing one with his AA secretary, Helen Wynn.

Bill believed in ghosts, Ouija boards and claims to have partaken in a gathering of spirits in Nantucket, MA, both seeing and conversing with up to 4 of these spirits at one time.

None of these things in and of themselves are enough to discredit his ideas. However, taken as a whole, they should give you pause before you decide to unquestioningly follow his program of recovery!

It's about underlying causes not moral weakness

For most people there are other underlying causes that have to be identified and solved in order to be freed from addiction. Those causes can range from a poor self-image, under-developed life skills, a distorted or false view of the world, or having suffered an extremely traumatic event. For those who started their addictive lifestyle at an early age, many never "grew up" and learned the skills necessary for handling the everyday stress and pitfalls of reality. I have met quite a few people who claim that their drinking never really caused them any major issues or problems to speak of. For them, so they say, drinking and partying was simply fun but that over time it got out of hand. While that may have been initially true, years of drinking alcoholically will inevitably create issues and cause mental dysfunction.

If you have tried AA and not found everlasting sobriety as a result, you are not a failure, loser or "unfortunate". It simply did not work for you. This does not mean that you are doomed to a life of drunkenness or drug addiction. It doesn't work for a lot of people for a lot of reasons. It's not your fault!

AA-The only game in town

It would be nice if we could make AA work for everybody because it is virtually the only game in town. If you go to a rehabilitation facility, the exit strategy and aftercare program suggested by virtually every last one of them is to immediately immerse yourself with AA. The same holds true if you go to a licensed drug and alcohol counselor. Hopefully if you go to see a psychiatrist or therapist, they will be able to help you discover and work through your underlying issues and pain and thus, render the whole AA experience as unnecessary.

Again, what about the people who have already found God, turned their lives over to him, are deeply religious but find themselves to be an alcoholic anyway? How are the steps supposed to help them? The same thing is true for the morally upstanding, loving and altruistic agnostic and secular people of the world. Chances are that they will simply not see the "white light" and for them the program is also a virtually impossible sell.

AA- A Bandage not a cure

Yes, AA can keep you sober but it's only a bandage. Clearly if you call your sponsor several times a day and go to meetings constantly you won't have time to drink. That's how it works! The problem is that by doing this you haven't necessarily addressed any of the underlying issues that drove you to addiction in the first place. The claimed success rate of AA is virtually impossible to verify due its very nature of anonymity. If it was even remotely as successful as it claims, then there wouldn't be nearly enough room in the church basements where most AA meetings take place. The majority of "new" people that I've witnessed coming into meetings are those that have tried before but for whatever reason "went back out" (this is the term used by members to describe those that have resumed their addictive pattern). Veterans of the

‹ to point out that in almost all of these cases
tion stopped going or drastically cut down
ind contact with others in the group. While
an blame them? The meetings aren't terribly
_____ ____ __ey are always the same. Yes it is true that by
not rigorously following a stringent AA schedule you are not
getting your daily dose of AA medicine. You are pulling the
bandage off. By all means keep the bandage on for as long as
you think you need it but at some point you may find that like
many other people, you want more out of life than simply
surviving and eking out sobriety. You want to be cured and it
is possible!!

The good news is that there are few good ideas and advice within the AA program and its philosophy that are useful
and that might help people get to the root of their problems.
Included here would be things such as acceptance, the group
therapy concept, compassion, understanding and many more.
I also think that a few of the 12 steps themselves, with some
re-wording, could be somewhat helpful.

For example, AA's 4th step, "Made a searching and fearless moral inventory of ourselves", begins to address the issue
of underlying causes but does not solve it. It concentrates on
the bad things we've done and our character flaws as opposed
to uncovering the issues or events that led one to this state. I
will say it again and again, until these causes have been resolved, I feel that relentless attendance of AA meetings, while
it may keep you sober, is only a Bandage not a cure. When
you really look at it, it is another form of addiction.

A brief qualification

Before going any further, not that it should matter, let me
state that I myself am a very spiritual person though not necessarily a formally religious one. To use the AA vernacular, I
will briefly "qualify" here as to why I have the "right" to pub-
lish and make these opinions public. My drinking odyssey

began on New Year's Eve, 1973 at the tender age of twelve and continued on until the age of 48 on July 4th, 2010. I am not a big fan of the rehashing of people's "stories", but again to prove that I belong in the conversation I will give you a brief rendition of my substance abuse history. Suffice it for now to state that my struggles with alcoholism cost me educational opportunities, the pursuit of artistic and athletic endeavors and most tragically my marriage and the love and respect of my children. I sincerely hope that through the passage of time, doing the next right thing, and through the power of love, that I will be able to make amends to those whom have suffered as a result.

My first experience with Alcoholics Anonymous was not voluntary as it was a court ordered condition as a result of my one and only arrest for driving while intoxicated. Although I knew deep down that drinking had been a problem for a long time, I was not ready to seek any other alternative to my quiet discontent in life other than through the drinking that I still thought was working just fine. I would find myself giving AA the old college try on at least three separate occasions since that time. While I must admit that some of what I observed and learned in the halls contributed to my sobriety, I have to honestly state that AA is not responsible for my present and continued sobriety. I am a huge supporter of the basic premise of the entity's twelfth step that states, "Having had a spiritual awakening as a result of these steps, we tried to carry this message to alcoholics, and to practice these principles in all our affairs". I believe in the idea of trying to help others but not in the following of the steps. The altruistic spirit and genuine affections towards their fellow man is undeniable in most of those who consider themselves to be a member of the fellowship of AA.

Mr. Wilson's intent was honorable. To quote another AA-ism, "Take what you need and leave the rest".

Chapter 2

Alcoholism is not a life sentence!

The old adage of once an alcoholic always an alcoholic is utter nonsense. You can be cured, yes I said cured, of any addiction! That is not to say that you can ever use alcohol or any drug to which you were once addicted ever again without the almost definite result of becoming re-addicted. Once you pick up again it is almost guaranteed that you will be off and running towards oblivion and destruction. What you can do is put your alcoholism or addiction into remission. At some point those who have suffered from dependency have crossed a line that most people mercifully never do and unfortunately there is no stepping back over. Whether it's been 10 days, 10 months or 10 years; it doesn't matter, you can't go back if you want to be assured of lasting sobriety. If you haven't indulged in your drug of choice for a period of time, you cannot logically still be classified as an addict or alcoholic. Are you still potentially walking on thin ice? Absolutely, but at this point neither you nor anybody else should be referring to you as an alcoholic, recovering or otherwise!

I must also add here that when I say cured, I'm not talking about just being able to abstain from your addictive substance. While abstinence ultimately is the answer, unless you are happy about the decision to permanently quit drinking, it probably won't last. There are those who through sheer willpower somehow manage to "white knuckle" it and stay away from alcohol or drugs for considerable periods of time. In AA jargon these folks are termed "dry drunks". Their feelings of discontent have not been alleviated so they still feel less than whole. Their relapse is virtually inevitable. AA's 12 steps do very little if anything to address the underlying causes of alcoholism. Your AA group can act as a 24/7 babysitter and keep you sober but unless you uncover your personal issues and address them, a true feeling of everlasting peace will very likely elude you.

You are not powerless!!!

Step one of Alcoholics Anonymous states that "We admitted we were powerless over alcohol-that our lives had become unmanageable." I'll agree that we managed to make our lives and of those around us miserable by our destructive and selfish behavior. At the end of the day, however, the ONLY one who has the power to overcome such an affliction is the individual who suffers from it. The statement itself shifts blame and responsibility away from the individual and puts it somewhere else. How convenient! Clearly nobody becomes an alcoholic on purpose. Step one is a bold statement that gives one permission to pass the buck and rely on someone (God or their sponsor) or something (The AA group or a rock) to resolve their crisis. This is not to say that you should not seek the help of others in confronting this dilemma but the initiative has to be yours. I think step one should be reworded somewhere along the lines of "We became aware of and accepted the fact that we had developed a potentially deadly problem and that we needed to address and overcome it-that our lives had become dysfunctional, selfish and unmanageable and that it was our responsibility to change it". In other words, we have a problem and we had better fix it or else we're going down! You have to acknowledge to yourself that it has become a major issue and be mature enough to realize that it is your responsibility to do what is necessary to recover. If your only motivation for seeking help is to appease your spouse, children or boss, the chances of your success are minimal at best. The desire or need for change has to come from within. I believe that acceptance goes one step beyond admission in that if you accept something, you are no longer in denial. You can admit something but not truly believe it.

You need to overcome denial to reach acceptance

If we can agree that acceptance is the first step on the road to recovery the next logical question is how do we get there? In Elisabeth Kubler's book, *On death and dying*, she identifies five stages of grief, starting with denial and ending in acceptance, that one goes through when experiencing a terrible loss. In the case of an alcoholic or addict, the loss of their coping mechanism, be it the bottle or drug of choice, is a very traumatic experience. In many cases they have alienated just about everyone in their life and their abused substance is the only friend they have left.

Again, the first step in this process of grieving is that of denial which is simply the opposite of acceptance; the rejection of reality and the truth. In the case of an alcoholic, mountains of evidence proving their dire condition are usually painfully clear to see, yet the individual either outright refuses to recognize them or he or she attempts to rationalize and justify them. Alcoholism is a slowly progressive condition in that it only gets worse over time and never better. Because of this gradual progression, many people can trudge along for many years as what has come to be known as "functioning alcoholics". The ramifications of their drinking have not yet caused the calamities that will inevitably make denial impossible. They haven't yet lost their jobs, friends, families or been involved in any automobile accidents. The key word here is yet, because as sure as the sun will rise, these are just some of the negative results that await every addict.

Anger, rationalization and justification

Denial also manifests itself in varying degrees. In its mildest form one might actually "admit" that there is a problem but with the caveat that it's not their fault. Here is where "powerlessness" becomes a convenient excuse. On the next level they again might admit there is an issue but state that they can stop whenever they want to. The most blatant form is outright denial in which the person flat out angrily states that there is no problem. Regardless of how severe the denial is, in all cases short of outright denial, there are always rationalizations or justifications given for why the obvious just can't be true. Quite simply, denial is a defense mechanism. It is the only way in which people can blind themselves to the impact or harm that they are causing to both themselves and those around them. They are in effect out of touch with the real world. It enables the alcoholic to avoid having any feelings of guilt or remorse and enables them to be oblivious of the truth. People caught in the web of addiction are in an extremely immature state in that they are not living life on life's terms. In early stages, before life has become "unmanageable", the individual may justify their behavior with such excuses as "it's legal and everybody does it" or "I'm not hurting anybody", etc. The list goes on and on! More often than not they will lie to themselves and to those around them without even realizing it. As the evidence starts to mount, they either don't care or have crossed the line and simply can't stop. When asked why they drink so much the answer is usually that it feels good and that they like it. Sadder still, some will say that they don't know why and don't even question why they consume alcohol in such a reckless manner when the rest of society can somehow do it in a moderate, mature and responsible way.

At a certain point in time, the ramifications of one's alcoholism become so glaringly apparent that denial is no longer viable. It just doesn't cut it anymore because even the individual can no longer buy into and justify the behavior. At this juncture one often moves to the next step in the process, which is that of anger.

There is a saying that the truth will set you free. While this is undoubtedly accurate, it could also be said that the ugly truth will piss you off! Now that you are no longer able to lie to yourself and deny the truth, the emotional floodgates are opened wide. Your coping mechanism has been stripped away and rendered ineffectual. You know that you have to change and you don't want to. Change is hard and it goes against basic human nature. It requires difficult work, discipline and developing a whole new way of living. "It's just not fair!" Here is where the blame game usually comes into play. Now the justifications are directed at outside factors. My parents didn't love me, I was raised in a poor and underprivileged situation, it's not my fault, etc… It is a uniquely human belief that life is supposed to go your way and when it doesn't you become angry. The rest of the animal kingdom doesn't suffer from this delusion. When the temperature plummets below freezing the jackrabbit doesn't lament that it isn't fair, it seeks shelter and deals with it. Life can be hard and that's just the way it is. You have to accept life on life's terms and accept reality. It's all a part of becoming mature and growing up. Frustration at this point becomes intolerable and one will usually try to go back into denial. The revealed truth of the situation, however, makes this a short lived endeavor and so the next stage, that of bargaining, comes into play.

Let's make a deal

For the alcoholic this may take the form of convincing oneself that he or she can cut back and drink only on weekends or to switch from vodka to beer. Maybe they will attempt to hide the problem and drink in secret telling themselves that they will be able to get a handle on it. None of it works, because as

I mentioned previously, you have crossed the line and moderation is no longer an option. An even more important reason for its futileness lies in the fact that you still haven't discovered or addressed any of the underlying causes that contributed to your becoming addicted in the first place. Desperation will lead one to beg and plead for forgiveness and to try to bargain for "just one more chance". Loving spouses, children and hopeful employers will often do just that in the hopes that the addict is sincere and really will get it together. This process can be painfully long and the results are almost always a failure.

I myself was stuck in the bargaining stage for years until my family had finally had enough and threw me out. Every time I made the impossible promise to put down the bottle it inevitably failed. Sometimes I would last several weeks or even months before my discontent drove me back. The saddest occasion occurred as I was approaching one year of sobriety. We were vacationing with friends on a beautiful lake in Maine and I was driving up separately after work to meet everybody up there. Somehow along the way I began justifying in my own mind how I somehow deserved or earned the right to pick up a bottle along the way. After all we were on vacation and I had been good for so long. Having arrived an hour or so before everybody else, I helped myself to several nice gulps and then proceeded to hide the bottle in the woods close to the summer house. Shortly after everyone arrived, the obsession for another shot reared its ugly head and took over. I snuck into the woods, on my hands and knees so as not to be seen, found the bottle and took a nice big slug. Unknown to me was the fact that my wife had gone back into the house to start unpacking in the bedroom that faced the woods and she saw the whole pathetic scene. She had actually baked a one year sobriety anniversary/celebration cake that she was going to surprise me with that very evening. Talk about blowing it big time. Time after time I picked the most inopportune times to fall off the wagon.

The edge of darkness

I finally ran out of chances and was shown the door. In hindsight she should have done it years before but for the children's sake, she kept giving me chance after chance with the desperate hope that I would come to my senses and see all that I was jeopardizing. I'm sure it was the hardest thing that she ever had to do in her life. She was at her wits end and just couldn't do it anymore. At that point there was no more negotiating or bargaining. Who could blame her? Somewhere she knew that deep down I was not a horrible person that wanted to emotionally hurt her or the kids but that was no longer enough. Remorse and guilt were no match for the grip that alcoholism had over me.

So I had finally pushed the envelope and found myself completely and utterly alone. With denial no longer viable and all bargaining off of the table, I was finally fully ensconced into the last stage of grieving before acceptance, depression. Keep in mind that depression can be present throughout the whole process, but once you've exhausted all of the other stages, it is pretty much all that is left. In my case, I had to go through the whole grieving process again due to the loss of my family as a result of my poor choices.

With acceptance comes hope

It is often in this hopeless state of depression where one's defenses are weakened to the point where acceptance will finally become viable. At this time, people have often reached what has been termed their "bottom". While some people can jump straight from denial to acceptance, in more cases than not, they go through most of these stages. Keep in mind that acceptance is by no means necessarily an end to depression! The good news is that where there is acceptance, there is hope and the possibility of recovery.

Chapter 3

Embrace life, not AA's guilt trip and program of lies

Ok, now that we've reached a stage of acceptance and have "admitted" to ourselves that we need to address our condition, what's the next step? As I stated in the forward, pretty much all roads, at least as suggested by the rehabilitation and recovery community, will lead one to AA.

One of AA's biggest lies that it preaches is the idea, that as an alcoholic, your only shot at salvation is to become a lifelong member of its organization. According to their way of thinking, one can never be cured of alcoholism. In their eyes, the best that one can hope to achieve is to keep it at bay "one day at a time" through complete submission to their 12 step program.

This view is stated very clearly at the beginning of virtually every AA meeting by the reading of a passage from their textbook or more accurately, from its holy scripture, *Alcoholics Anonymous*. This AA manual, published by the organization but largely attributed to the writing of Bill Wilson, is lovingly referred to by its members as the "Big Book" and that is how I will refer to it going forward. The information contained within is considered gospel and to even remotely question any of its ideas is considered blasphemy by the AA community.

The passage is taken from the beginning of Chapter 5 (4th addition, page 58) which is titled, "How it works". It really amounts to a nifty guilt provoking sales pitch and it implies that unless you are a complete idiot, you will embrace AA's wonderful way of life. The first paragraph reads as follows;

How it works is a lie!

"Rarely have we seen a person fail who has thoroughly followed our path. Those who do not recover are people who cannot or will not completely give themselves to this simple program, usually men and women who are constitutionally incapable of being honest with themselves. There are such unfortunates. They are not at fault; they seem to have been born that way. They are naturally incapable of grasping and developing a manner of living which demands rigorous honesty."

WOW! What an incredibly arrogant, insulting and patently false statement! The first sentence is a lie. I have personally witnessed hundreds of people coming back to AA after having failed even though they; "followed the steps, called their sponsors, etc." A sponsor is a personal mentor that one picks from the group to help guide them through the 12 steps of the program. Old school AA disciples will usually point out that these people had cut down on their attendance of meetings and did not keep in daily contact with their sponsors and that is why they relapsed.

So in other words, unless you take your daily dose of AA medicine you will inevitably fail. For those that have not discovered and addressed their underlying issues that caused them to drink in the first place, this is probably true. This statement also insinuates that once you have joined the AA flock and found salvation that you had better not leave or else you are doomed. If this doesn't reek of a fundamental religious power play then I don't know what does. This is where the true TRAGEDY of AA lies. When you give AA a try because psychiatrists, counselors, members of the AA organization and society as a whole tell you that it is virtually the only solution and then it doesn't work for you, then you are bound to become hopeless and give up any serious attempt at recovery!

I'm absolutely sure that I am not the only one who left the "fellowship" demoralized and resigned to the fact that I was destined to live out my life depressed and drunk. I feel extremely confident that the number of people who invariably took this route by far exceeds those who have found and maintained sobriety through AA's church and 12-Step religion.

The second sentence in this self-righteous paragraph implies that if you can't get with the program that you are a dishonest and hopeless liar! Quite the nerve there!

For the longest time I thought that the third line was a typo and that the word "there" was actually supposed be "they're", as in "they are such unfortunates". NO, the intent actually is to say; "Wow, can you believe that there are actually people who don't get and embrace this?" Well yes, there are lots of them.

While it is obvious that those inflicted with addiction are in denial and are lying to themselves about the extent of their dilemma, I find it reprehensible to insinuate that anybody is incapable of choosing to seek the truth and take responsibility for the direction of their life without an affiliation with AA.

Life is what it is, act accordingly

To Alcoholics Anonymous' credit, the organization does recognize the importance of acceptance as is evidenced by the fact that virtually all of its meetings close with what has become known as The Serenity Prayer. Granted, some meetings adjourn with the Lord's Prayer or that of St. Francis but I would say that over ninety percent do so with The Serenity Prayer. Hmmm, doesn't AA claim to be non-religious? Anyway, I digress. AA's version goes like this; "God, grant me the serenity to accept the things I cannot change, courage to change the things I can, and the wisdom to know the difference."

Something about the 2nd half of the prayer always bothered me but it took me some time to put my finger on it. After doing some research on the subject, my intuition for what was wrong with it was confirmed for me. For some reason, AA in its infinite wisdom changed the prayer from the way it was originally written. That version, penned by the well-known theologian and political thinker, Ronald Niebuhr, goes as follows; "God, give us the grace to accept with serenity the things that cannot be changed, courage to change the things that should be changed, and the wisdom to distinguish the one from the other." Before I examine the fundamental difference between using the word *can* instead of *should* as far as changing things is concerned, let me first discuss the first part of the prayer in which both AA and I are in agreement.

Accepting things that can't be changed is the only mature and rational response to reality. The alternative of denial as previously discussed is not a terribly healthy or sane choice. It is in our nature to resist change and continue doing what is known and therefore comfortable and not dangerous to our ego. Acceptance means that you acknowledge the world as it is right now, regardless of whether or not it is as you would like it to be!

Could have, would have, should have

The saying, "could have, would have, should have", is very useful in pointing out and deciphering some of the thoughts that are often present when trying to accept the reality and ramifications of your actions. Events may take place and you may think to yourself that if you could go back, that you would have or could have done something differently and therefore the results would have been more favorable. Acceptance means understanding that that ship has passed and that you can't "undo" what is done. It is what it is!

Now as far as the "should have" goes; here is where you

still may have a chance to "set things right". Maybe you didn't initially do the right thing or take the best course of action but maybe it isn't too late! This is where the second part of Niebuhr's version of The Serenity Prayer comes into play. You may very well have the opportunity to "change the things that you *should* try and change". Of course there are no guarantees that any new course of action will bring about the desired results, but at least you tried to do the right thing. After these attempts of making sound choices and trying to undo past harm are exhausted, then you need to accept the final results. If you don't, you are going to get caught up in resentments, self-pity or fear, none of which are good for your mental state of health.

They should have left it alone

AA's version of the second verse of the Prayer, which states that we should change the things that we *can*, is fundamentally flawed. I'm sure that wasn't their intent but they should have left the original version intact. The problem here is that we *can* change a whole plethora of things and make them even worse! We can also effect change that might benefit ourselves but that is hurtful to others or that is just plain immoral.

Just because you *can* does NOT mean that you *should*!

Let me make up a little hypothetical story here just to make my point. John is the controller of a small family business owned by the Ortega family and he handles virtually every financial aspect of the company's affairs. Because they like him and English is their second language, the Ortegas have complete faith and trust in John and never question in the least any financial statements or opinions that he offers. Recently John's family has suffered through financial hardships due to his wife having been laid off from her job and his son having begun college. They have missed two payments on their mortgage and the bank is threatening foreclosure. Although John loves and respects the Ortegas greatly, his mind starts conniving ways in which he can skim some money to save his home. He cooks the books and does just that, while jeopardizing the solvency of the Ortega's family business. Obviously he was put in the position whereby he COULD do this. SHOULD he have? Of course not, it was both illegal and immoral! He should have gotten a second job, negotiated with the bank, sent his son to community college or come up with a legal solution to his dilemma.

The last part of the prayer says that we should have the WISDOM to know the difference. Knowing the difference between what we can't change (the acceptance part) and the courage to change the things we can (the change part), isn't rocket science. The true WISDOM is in the decision to change the things that we SHOULD, if we can when appropriate. Again, while I believe that AA really had Niebuhr's intention in mind, they should have left the wording just as it was.

As an alcoholic, you must accept the seriousness of your present condition and the need to change your future reality

As far as addiction goes, we must accept the fact that we have crossed the line and that we need to address the situation. We do not have to accept the notion that we are such "unfortunates"!

Change is not only necessary, it is inevitable and good

AA uses a lot of slogans in meetings, most of which I would imagine are borrowed but are generally good advice for anybody. Don't get me wrong, some are absolutely horrible but one that is fitting here goes like this; "Nothing changes if nothing changes". While this might sound very simplistic, it really isn't. In more cases than not a whole new way of approaching life is going to be needed if you seriously want to get well. It might mean not seeing people that you used hang out with. It might mean that going to the bar after the softball game is not such a great idea. Someday you might be able socialize with these people and do those things but initially I would highly recommend not doing so. Chances are that at the outset you're going to be anxious, vulnerable and not at all sure of yourself. As time goes on, you will find that being around those who are able to partake in social drinking is no longer an issue. Understand, however, that it might take a little while. Be kind to yourself and don't put unnecessary pressure on the process. Choosing sobriety is hard and you will undoubtedly feel that it is unfair but you can and will change for the better. Sober living is FUN! I actually remember what I did yesterday, enjoy the moment today and look forward to tomorrow. You don't need a 12-Step program to do this but rather, you need to embrace a new way of thinking and approaching life. That's what part two of this book is all about. The remaining chapters of this half of the book will trace AA's history, its approach and point out both its pros and cons.

Chapter 4

How the bizarre 12 step religion came to be

Before getting into the heart of AA's 12 steps, a little AA history is in order. Because Bill Wilson was the author of said steps and the clear leader and inspiration for the entire AA movement, I feel that it is necessary to take a closer look at a few traumatic events that occurred and the overall tone of his life during his formative years. Furthermore, I will examine what was going on in his life at the time when this whole movement came to fruition.

Bill was born in the fall of 1895 in the town of East Dorsett, Vermont. When he was only ten years old his parents separated, divorced and then abandoned him. His father, Gilman Wilson, had been a heavy drinker and was having an adulterous affair. Although Bill swore that this would not be his legacy, he would eventually follow the same exact path. After the divorce, Gilman moved to Canada to work at a marble quarry. Less than a year later his mother, Emily, decided that she wanted to pursue a medical education and career in Boston, Massachusetts. Prior to her decision to move for a fresh start, she had had a series of nervous breakdowns.

A sad pattern emerges

As a result of this family upheaval, Bill and his younger sister, Dorothy, were left to be raised by his maternal grandparents. It was at about this time that Bill would suffer from the first of what would become a lifetime series of battles with depression. His grandparents were church-going folks and tried to indoctrinate Bill into a religious way of life. However, due to the sense of abandonment that he suffered at the hands of his parents, he soon decided that there could not possibly be a loving God in the universe and declared that he had become an atheist.

Bill's life took a turn for the better when his grandfather, Fayette Griffith, made the decision to send him to Burr and Burton, an exclusive boarding school in Manchester, Vermont. Most of the student body came from wealthy families and initially Bill felt awkward and out of place. As time went on though, his confidence soared and he excelled in everything from football and track to acting and playing the violin. By his junior year he was enjoying what he would later reminisce as to being the best time of his life. He was voted class president and met and fell in love with a very pretty and popular girl, Bertha Bramford. Unfortunately for Bill, his sense of being on top of the world would be very short lived. In the fall of his senior year, Bertha was taken to Flower Hospital in New York City to have a small tumor removed. She died on the operating room table and Bill's world came crashing down. He once again sank into a depression so severe that he quit all of his extra-curricular activities, was failing most of his classes and did not graduate with his peers.

Things were so bleak that even his absentee mother tried to intervene and get him back on track. She had him move in with her outside of Boston to finish high school with the lofty ambition of having him then move on to the Massachusetts Institute of Technology (M.I.T.) to earn a degree in engineering. Unfortunately Bill was still in such a depressive funk that he couldn't pull it off.

At her wits end, Emily sent Bill up to Canada to visit his father to see if the change of scenery would do him some good. Gilman was well entrenched in his position as supervisor of a quarry, had met a new woman and was very busy establishing a new life for himself. While he was glad that his son had come to visit, he just really didn't have time for what he considered to be a part of his past. With Canada clearly not being the answer, Bill returned to his grandparents in East Dorset.

It was back in Vermont where Bill would meet Lois Burham, whom he would later marry. Lois was the daughter of a prominent doctor from Brooklyn, NY who owned several summer houses in the Vermont countryside. When Lois returned to Brooklyn for the fall, Bill gave further education one more chance when he enrolled at Norwich University, a military college located in the heart of Vermont. Depression and anxiety again got the best of him and he never finished his second semester. Bill would repeat this attempt with the same result the following fall when Lois again returned to Brooklyn.

Bill finds relief in the bottle

Bill's life was forever changed when the United States entered the fray of World War One and he was drafted. It was while being stationed at Fort Rodman in New Bedford, Massachusetts, that he started attending high society parties in nearby Newport, Rhode Island and discovered the effects of alcohol. As it does for so many people, booze instantly removed his anxiety and feelings of inferiority. Like so many an alcoholic before and since, he was more or less instantly addicted.

Bill and Lois were married on January 24th, 1918 and settled into a teeny apartment in New Bedford. He was finally sent abroad to join the war effort that spring but he never saw any actual combat and finally returned to Brooklyn with Lois after the war ended and they moved in with her parents. Bill's drinking continued to escalate and he had extreme difficulties in ever holding a job for more than a few months. He went back to school and earned his law degree but he never practiced. He was offered a job by Thomas Edison but that would have required working real hours and actually commuting to New Jersey every day which was a sacrifice that Bill was not willing to make. Meanwhile, Lois supported the two of them working long hours in retail.

If you talk to most folks in AA, all they know of Bill's work history is that he was a wildly successful Wall Street analyst and investor. While he did prosper there for a few years from about 1927 up until the crash in 1929, he still never even amassed enough wealth to buy his own home while the truly successful investors were building massive estates in the Hamptons, the Gold Coast of Long Island and places like Greenwich, Connecticut. After the stock market crash, Bill again could not hold onto any meaningful employment, his drinking escalated to even higher levels and once again he and Lois were forced to move back into her parents' home.

The seeds of Alcoholics Anonymous

By 1933 Bill was drinking around the clock and at the urging of family and friends he checked into the Charles B. Towns Hospital for his first attempt at rehabilitation. As is the case for most addicts, the initial attempt lasted only a few weeks. If nothing else, this experience led Bill to accept the inescapable reality of his problem and led to his sincere desire for help. Between this episode and his final stay at Towns, when he experienced his drug induced religious conversion, several other critical experiences helped shape Bill's ideas that led to the formation of Alcoholics Anonymous.

The first of these was Bill's introduction to the Oxford Group, a Christian religious organization founded by a Lutheran minister, Frank Buchman, which had had marginal success in helping alcoholics achieve mostly short term reprieves from their drinking. Wilson himself would admit that the bulk of his 12 steps and AA's general philosophy came directly from the teachings and ideology of the Oxford Group.

A prime example of this would be in the way that he incorporated the four practices that Buchman felt were necessary to become spiritually reborn. These can be found in the book; *What is the Oxford Group*, by The layman with a notebook, with a foreword by L.W. Grensted. The first of these practices is; "The sharing of our sins and temptations with another Christian life given to God, and to use Sharing as Witness to help others, still unchanged, to recognize and acknowledge their sins." This is pretty much a mirror of AA's fifth step of confession which is as follows; "Admitted to God, to ourselves, and to another human being the exact nature of our wrongs". This practice is also a predominant element in almost all AA meetings where one member shares his or her "experience, strength and hope" with the others. The format and content of the various types of meetings will be discussed in a subsequent chapter.

The next practice indicates that we should "Surrender our life past, present and future, into God's keeping and direction". AA's third step is virtually identical to this and is reworded as follows; "Made a decision to turn our will and our lives over to the care of God as we understood him".

The third practice; "Restitution to all whom we have wronged directly or indirectly" directly parallels AA's eighth step; "Made a list of all persons we had harmed, and became willing to make amends to them all."

The last of these spiritual practices stresses "Listening to, accepting, relying on God's Guidance and carrying it out in everything we do or say, great or small". This is the basis of both steps eleven and twelve which go as follows-Step 11-"Sought through prayer and meditation to improve our conscious contact with God as we understood Him, praying only for knowledge of His will for us and the power to carry that out." Step 12-Having had a spiritual awakening as the result of these steps; we tried to carry this message to alcoholics, and to practice these principles in all our affairs.

Another major source of inspiration for Bill came from the reading of William James' book, *The Varieties of Reli-*

gious Experience. James, a well renowned psychologist, philosopher and Harvard professor, gave a series of lectures on the subject of religion at Edinburgh College in 1901-02 and the transcripts of these would later become the "Varieties". In the body of this work James cites various examples of people who experience a sudden religious conversion similar to the one that Bill Wilson claims to have experienced during his final stay at Towns Hospital. It is unclear whether he read the book before or after his experience but either way it clearly had a profound effect on his belief system.

AA's initial call to action, the second step, "Came to believe that a power greater than ourselves could restore us to sanity", comes directly from one of the last things that James had to say on the whole subject. I quote; "Meanwhile the practical needs and experiences of religion seem to me sufficiently met by the belief that beyond each man and in a fashion continuous with him there exists a larger power which is friendly to him and to his ideals. All that the facts require is that the power be both other and larger than our conscious selves. Anything larger will do, if only it be large enough to trust for the next step". That next step in Bill's mind is obviously that of surrendering to God in the third step. This should be sufficient evidence to state unequivocally that AA is religious in nature!

The final piece to the AA puzzle came together when Bill traveled to Akron, Ohio, on another failed business venture. While in Akron, Bill contacted some Oxford members and was introduced to Dr. Robert Smith (Dr. Bob), AA's other credited co-founder. As time went on, the Oxford Group became disenchanted with trying to help those with drinking problems because they were unruly in meetings and more often than not returned to drinking after only short periods of sobriety. Bill and Bob decided to take on the cause and on June 10, 1935 AA was born.

Chapter 5

AA's insane and faulty 12-step logic

Although the subsequent steps say otherwise, let's go with AA's initial premise that God is not necessarily the power needed that is greater than ourselves to begin the journey into sobriety. For most people that do not experience a sudden religious epiphany, that power usually manifests itself as a belief that the fellowship of AA and its group consciousness will serve that purpose.

OK, so back to AA's 2nd step which states; "Came to believe that a Power greater than ourselves could restore us to sanity". Hey, you may be messed up but you're not insane! People in AA love to quote Albert Einstein's definition of insanity which is as follows; "Doing the same thing over and over again and expecting different results". Honestly I don't think that people who are abusing alcohol or drugs are expecting anything other than getting high. In fact those are the exact results that they are seeking and not a whole lot of expectation or thinking is involved!

All right, to be fair, abusing alcohol or drugs is a bit crazy. To be sane is to be rational and clearly those who are abusing drugs and alcohol are not acting terribly rationally. Quite frankly, by the time most people reach this point, I don't think that they really care. In order to be rational, one needs to be mature, emotionally and mentally healthy and realistic. Yes, you might need some help to attain these traits but some mystical power greater than yourself is not the answer. The power is within all of us and we just need the desire to tap into and develop it. Addictive behavior is ego driven and selfish in nature. You need to embrace the fact that the world is not all about you. Some argue that they were shy and that drinking made them more social. I would argue that while alcohol does reduce inhibitions it hardly makes you more social. It makes you more talkative often to the point of being annoying and obnoxious. Inebriated people almost always want to be the center of attention. People under the influence might hear what other people are saying but rarely are they actively listening. A real conversation involves not only listening to the person, but actually caring about what they have to say. Active listening is a skill that does not come over night but it can and must be learned and developed. I'll discuss this in further detail in the 2nd half of the book.

Let the contradictions begin

In the chapter titled Step 2 in the book *Twelve Steps and Twelve Traditions,* (primarily written by Bill Wilson and often referred to as the 12 & 12) the following paragraph is forever quoted by AA members;

"First, Alcoholics Anonymous does not demand that you believe anything. All of its Twelve Steps are but suggestions. Second, to get sober and to stay sober, you don't have to swallow all of the steps right now. Looking back, I find that I took it piecemeal myself. Third, all you really need is a truly open mind. Just resign yourself from the debating society and quit bothering yourself with such deep questions as whether it was the hen or the egg that came first. Again I say, all you need is the open mind."

Well which is it? The first sentence says that you don't have to believe but is then immediately followed by statements that insinuate that you had better swallow them eventually or you have no chance of staying sober! Having an open mind means that while you are willing to consider all opinions, you then come to your own conclusions. To "resign yourself from the debating society", is in essence saying that you should not question any of these ideas but rather, to accept them as inarguable truths. These are far from being suggestions, they are commandments! Again the message here is that if you don't play along and adopt the 12 step religion, you might as well resign yourself to the fact that you won't get well.

On page 27 Bill suggests that; "You can, if you wish, make AA itself your 'higher power'". In other words, make the AA church and its religion your God. He goes on further to state that "All of them will tell you that, once across, their faith broadened and deepened. Relieved of the alcohol obsession, their lives unaccountably transformed, they came to believe in a Higher Power, and most of them began to talk of God."

This is the bridge that takes us from step 2 to that of step 3 which states; "Made a decision to turn our wills and our lives over to the care of God as we understood Him."

It must be noted here that Bill Wilson flip flops between the higher power as God or the AA group constantly and inserts one or the other depending on what argument he is trying to make. A perfect example of this is the fact that God is mentioned no less than 21 times in the eight and a half page chapter dealing with Step 2! He does it again in the 2nd paragraph of the chapter titled Step 3 (page 34), where he states; "Like all the remaining Steps, Step 3 calls for affirmative action, for it is only by action that we can cut away the self-will which has always blocked the entry of God-or if you like, a Higher Power-into our lives".

Bizarre Logic

Just how can you consider turning your will and your life over to either AA or to God as affirmative action? It is just the opposite. Cutting away your self-will really just means turning over responsibility for your life over to someone or something else. He further reinforces his absurd argument on page 36 where he states; "The more we become willing to depend upon a Higher Power, (take your pick here) the more independent we actually are. Therefore dependence, as A.A. practices it, is really a means of gaining true independence of the spirit". Immediately following this irrational thought, Bill goes on to make a bizarre analogy comparing being dependent on a Higher Power to that of being dependent on electricity for modern conveniences and that these wonderful electronic inventions thus enable us to be more independent. One has nothing to do with the other and the bottom line is that if you become more dependent on anything, you by definition are losing a degree of independence.

Further along he negatively exhorts; "How persistently we claim the right to decide all by ourselves just what we shall think and just how we will act".

I feel that as long as we are behaving both legally and in a morally just way, are these not rights accorded to us in our very own constitution? I guess we should forsake these basic rights and just let AA and our sponsors dictate our life. I really don't think so! Following Bill's "suggestions" leads one away from independence rather than towards it. Mr. Wilson's arguments and logic are often faulty and contradictory.

Again I just want to state here that I am not trying to make a case either for or against organized religion but I do feel the need to quote from page 30 of this same chapter simply because it left me shaking my head; "How we loved to shout the damaging fact that millions of the 'good men of religion' were still killing one another off in the name of God. This all meant, of course, that we had substituted negative for positive thinking".

Say what?! Is there something negative about feeling that it is wrong for millions of people to have died because they had differing religious beliefs? No further comment needed here.

Recovery should not be about religion

Following an organized religion is fine and if it brings peace and direction to your life, then that's fantastic. That being said, being religious is not necessarily going to solve your addiction. Just ask the millions of alcoholics who attend church regularly.

Bill of course has an answer as to why there are some people who consider themselves devoutly religious but for some reason are still prisoners of addiction. His simple answer is that they are obviously practicing their faith poorly. While it is true that just showing up for church does not make you a morally sound person, going to AA meetings and listening to people's stories isn't necessarily going to change that. Even if it did, that does not necessarily address the underlying causes of your addiction.

Whether your higher power is God, AA, or a rock, the message that Bill Wilson is sending here is clear. In order to overcome your alcoholism you must surrender to the AA church and God and follow the 12 commandments-oops, I mean steps!

AA's unwavering stance regarding this is clearly stated on pages 44 and 45 of the Big Book where Bill states that if you are an alcoholic then;

"You may be suffering from an illness which only a spiritual experience will conquer. To be doomed to an alcoholic death or to live on a spiritual basis are not always easy alternatives to face. But after a while we had to face the fact that we must find a spiritual basis of life-or else. Perhaps it is going to be that way with you. But cheer up, something like half of us thought we were atheists or agnostics. Our experience shows you need not be disconcerted. If a mere code of morals or a better philosophy of life were sufficient to overcome alcoholism, many of us would have recovered long ago. We could wish to be moral, we could wish to be philosophically comforted, in fact, we could will these things with all our

might, but the needed power wasn't there. Our human resources, as marshaled by the will, were not sufficient; they
failed utterly."

WRONG, WRONG, WRONG!

Sure, wishing to have higher morals and a better philosophy
or understanding of life is not enough, you have to learn and
work for it! You do, in fact, possess free will and it is your responsibility to utilize it to make the decision to improve these
areas of your life.

Further proof that AA is a religion is expressed by Bill on
page 49 where he states; "We who have traveled this dubious
path, beg you to lay aside prejudice, even against organized
religion. We have learned that whatever the human frailties of
various faiths may be; those faiths have given purpose and direction to millions. People of faith have a logical idea of what
life is all about".

Say what?

Faith is an unquestioning belief which is the exact opposite of
using logic to come to a conclusion. He expands on this faulty
reasoning again when he says; "Without knowing it, had we
not been brought to where we stood by a certain kind of faith?
For did we not believe in our own reasoning? Did we not
have confidence in our ability to think? What is that but a sort
of faith? Yes we had been faithful, abjectly faithful to the God
of Reason. So, in one way or another, we discovered that faith
had been involved all along!"

Again, confidence and dependence in our ability to think
is the polar opposite of blind faith! Do you see how he twists
things? Mr. Wilson was the consummate spin doctor!

On page 45 Bill says; "Lack of power, that was our dilemma. We had to find a power greater than ourselves.
Obviously. But where and how were we to find this Power?"

I'm sorry but I don't think that this line of reasoning is obvious to anybody. The power to alter your life's direction is yours and yours alone. Free will and the ability to think for ourselves is what separates us as human beings from the marvelous creatures of the animal kingdom that make decisions based on instinct alone. If you don't want to become a sheep in the AA flock, then you don't have to.

Finally, Bill sums it all up by stating; "Well, that's exactly what this book is about. Its main object is to enable you to find a Power greater than yourself which will solve your problem."

Let me state here that I believe that most of the organized religions of the world share and preach some very important and desirable ways in which one should live their life. Included here would be such things as forgiveness, altruism, empathy, compassion, and the idea that we should "Do unto others as you would have others do unto you". The thing is that you don't have to be part of any organized religion or AA in order to strive for these ideals. No God or Higher Power is needed in order to *do the right thing*.

If you want to turn over your will and life to God, I recommend studying to become a pastor or a priest. If you want to give up your individuality and independence to God or the AA group, be prepared to live a peaceful but mundane and non-questioning life as a sheep in the AA flock.

Make the right decision!

The first three words of Step 3 are "Made a decision". At this point you clearly have to ask yourself some serious questions and you do have to make some very important decisions. Surrendering and turning over your will and life, however, are not answers that you should accept!

Part two of the book will deal with how to heal yourself, live better and have a more fulfilling life without necessarily having to rely on God, AA or any other higher power.

In the next chapter we will take a look at what AA suggests as a course of action besides just changing your belief system.

Chapter 6

AA's sin list and confession

Alcoholics Anonymous' 4th step, "Made a searching and fearless moral inventory of ourselves", is at least an attempt at trying to uncover the reasons that have led people to their addictions. The problem is that it is more concerned with identifying your character defects rather than discovering the underlying causes. It concentrates heavily on the things that you've done wrong in life. There are some very useful points in Mr. Wilson's chapter regarding this step but for the most part the end result is that you come up with a SIN list. This is necessary because AA's 5th step, "Admitted to God, to ourselves, and to another human being the exact nature of our wrongs" is nothing more than a confession of said sins.

Bill blames it all on misguided instincts

Bill's chapter on Step 4 begins with the premise that all serious emotional problems are a direct result of our misdirected instincts. According to him, practically all of man's troubles are caused by unhealthy desires for sex, material possessions and emotional security. Just because these were all major "issues" in Bill's life, does not mean that they, with the possible exception of emotional maturity, are the cause for most people's addictions. Bill clearly felt guilt about his numerous adulterous affairs, his dependence on his wife and in-laws to support him and was clearly left emotionally insecure as a result of the abandonment by his parents that he suffered as a child. On page 43 of "Twelve Steps and Twelve Traditions", Bill states;

"How frequently we see a frightened human being determined to depend completely upon a stronger person for guidance and protection. This weak one, failing to meet life's responsibilities with his own resources, never grows up". Finally Bill identifies what may be an underlying cause for some people. This dependence and lack of maturity is very common, particularly for those whose addictive patterns began at a young age.

Bill further observes; "Alcoholics especially should be able to see that instinct run wild in themselves is the underlying cause of their destructive drinking. We have drunk to drown feelings of fear, frustration, and depression. We have drunk to escape the guilt of passions, and then have drunk again to make more passions possible".

Taking away his guilt for adultery, I agree that people drink due to fear, frustration and depression. These feelings, with the exception of fear caused by danger, however, are all caused by something other than instinct!

He goes on to say; "By now the newcomer has probably arrived at the following conclusions; that his character defects, representing instincts gone astray, have been the primary cause of his drinking". The only way most people would come to these strange conclusions is if he or she read and believed Bill's book or if his or her sponsor told them so.

Where Bill gets it right

One area in which I agree with Bill is the observation that emotional insecurity often reveals itself in the forms of worry, anger, self-pity and depression. Many addicts and alcoholics have a hard time dealing with life the way it is and have not developed the skills necessary to cope with the everyday stresses of life. It is true that many alcoholics are extremely self-centered and have a hard time forging healthy relationships with people.

Another area in which I am in total agreement with AA is the idea that you need to acknowledge, confront and move past any simmering resentments that you may be holding onto. You need to learn how to forgive both others and yourself. On page 66 of the "Big Book", Bill observes; "It is plain that a life which includes deep resentment leads only to futility and unhappiness. To the precise extent that we permit these, do we squander the hours that might have been worthwhile." Letting go of these resentments is of course often easier said than done. What about those who have suffered physical, mental or sexual abuse? These are clearly traumatizing events that can absolutely be one of the primary underlying causes for one's addiction. To live by the religious ideal of, "forgive thy enemy", is often just too much to ask. What I do know is that if you don't in some way confront and move past these life altering events, that they will continue to torment you. Professional counseling may very well be needed to address these kinds of issues.

Installing guilt is not a healthy answer

So how does one take his own inventory or create his sin list? Bill suggests that; "Using his best judgment of what has been right and what has been wrong, he might make a rough survey of his conduct with respect to his primary instincts for sex, security, and society" (Page 50 of 12 & 12).

On page 64 (Big Book) Bill suggests that; "we listed people, institutions or principles with which we were angry. We asked ourselves why we were angry." On the next page, suggested questions regarding these issues that we should ask ourselves include; "Where had we been selfish, dishonest, self-seeking and frightened?" You should look for where you were to blame and to observe your faults.

Now that you've made your list, what do you do with it? Bill states that; "We must be willing to make amends where we have done harm, provided that we do not bring about still more harm in so doing." I completely agree with this premise and steps 8-10 deal with this whole issue.

Confession does not make your "stuff" disappear!

Finally, Bill says; "If we are sorry for what we have done, and have the honest desire to let God take us to better things, we believe we will be forgiven and will have learned our lesson."

So there you have it. Confess ye sinners and all is right in the world. This is the transition that leads us to step 5; "Admitted to God, to ourselves and to another human being the exact nature of our wrongs". For the diehard AA'ers who still want to deny that the 5th step is the equivalent of the Catholic Church's practice of confession, I need only once again quote from page 56 of the 12 & 12 where Bill states; "They always discovered that relief never came by confessing the sins of other people. Everybody had to confess his own." Ok, point made, but the more important question to ask is; Does admitting and confessing your less than exemplary past misdeeds to somebody absolve you of them and more importantly, will it keep you from drinking? According to Bill, if you don't share your humiliating, distressing and guilty past, then you will either be unable to stay sober at all or at best have continuous relapses. Unless you confess, you will continue to suffer from the likes of irritability, anxiety, remorse, and depression. So, confessing all of your dirty little secrets to your sponsor is going to make those feelings disappear? There is absolutely no evidence to support this hypothesis whatsoever!

On the same page Bill goes on to further state that; "This practice of admitting one's defects to another person are, of course, very ancient. It has been validated in every century, and it characterizes the lives of all spiritually centered and truly religious people." Really? If you ask most Buddhists, Muslims, Jews or other people who consider themselves spiritual, I don't think any of them will tell you that they consider confession as an essential ingredient that characterizes their lives!

Granted, both the church and AA stress the point that if one's confession is not sincere and if there is no attempt to right one's wrongs, then it is not valid. Some wrongs can't be righted and just because you say or confess that that is your intent doesn't mean that it really is. Churches and AA halls are filled with Sunday "sinners" that go back to their ways as soon as they leave the confessional or their 5th step meeting!

It takes more than being "sorry"

The bottom line here folks is that we should clearly all try our best to right past wrongs and to do the next right thing (steps 8-10). My major problem with steps 4 & 5 is the heavy emphasis on guilt and the concentration on "character defects" as opposed to underlying causes. AA implies that if you uncover all the dirt and apologize to the world, that you will be relieved of these issues and be free. It just doesn't work that way. The key is to not only uncover your character defects, issues, underlying causes or whatever you want to call them, but to then learn how to change these traits and behaviors into more mature, mentally healthy and socially acceptable ways of being. In order to accomplish this there are certain things that must be done.

1-You have to admit (accept) that the way in which you are presently living your life is unhealthy, unproductive and selfish.

2- You have to truly want to get better and evolve into a more complete human being.

3- You have to objectively look at your past and take responsibility for learning from it and incorporating new ways of approaching life.

4- You have to be willing to not only learn the life skills necessary for healthier living but to actually apply them on a continual basis.

5- Lastly, you need to forgive yourself and know that all of these things are not only possible but that they are within YOUR POWER to be accomplished.

Before we get to how to accomplish these goals in Part 2 of the book, let's take a look at the remaining steps and then see what actually goes on at AA meetings.

Chapter 7

Don't become an AA sheep

AA's chapters 6; "Were entirely ready to have God remove all these defects of character", and 7; "Humbly asked Him to remove our shortcomings" are very straight forward and don't require a whole lot of commentary. You either believe that God is going to fix you and relieve you of your addictions or you don't. Chances are that if you thought that it was that easy, you wouldn't still be here reading.

In the Big Book, Bill says very little on these 2 steps because clearly they are a matter of faith. In the 12 & 12, on page 63 he says; "Of course, the often disputed question of whether God can-and will, under certain conditions-remove defects of character will be answered with a prompt affirmative by almost any AA member. To him, this proposition will be no theory at all; it will be just about the largest fact in his life." Further down on the same page he continues with; "But when I became willing to clean house and then asked a Higher Power, God as I understood Him, to give me release, my obsession to drink vanished."

Poof, it's gone! For most of us, it's just not that easy.

Bill's chapter on Step 7 in the 12 & 12 (page 70) is all about humility and starts off as follows; "Since this Step so specifically concerns itself with humility, we should pause here to consider what humility is and what the practice of it can mean to us. Indeed, the attainment of greater humility is the foundation principle of each of AA's Twelve Steps."

The *Dictionary.com* website defines humility as the condition of being humble; modest opinion or estimate of one's own importance, rank, etc... Synonyms cited include low-liness, meekness and submissiveness. Furthermore, when using the word humble as a verb (used with object), diction-ary.com defines to do so as;

    1 - to lower in condition, importance or dignity; abase.

    2 - to destroy the independence, power or will of.

    3 - to make meek: *to humble one's heart.*

Sheep breeding 101

Of course greater humility is the foundation of AA's reli-gion!!! You clearly have to become meek and give up your willpower in order to become a sheep in good standing. Don't get the wrong idea that I am advocating behaving like an ar-rogant ego maniac who places himself above all others. We are all part of a larger social world filled with other people and it is our responsibility to be a cooperative, empathetic and caring part of that world. In other words, we should all play nice! That being said, we should not become unquestioning robots that accept everything that is handed to us. Self-determination, free will and the ability to think is what sepa-rates us from sheep.

Hey I like sheep, they're cute but I don't want to be one!

Once again it is hard to get away from AA's religious ob-session when one considers Christianity's definition of humility which as stated on *Wikipedia's* website is as follows; "A quality by which a person considering his own defects has a humble opinion of himself and willingly submits himself to God and to others for God's sake." Bill comes pretty close to this definition when he says on page 72 (12&12); "As long as we placed self-reliance first, a genuine reliance upon a Higher Power was out of the question. That basic ingredient of all humility, a desire to seek and do God's will, was missing."

It all again comes down to the fact, in Bill's mind any-way, that we are all defective, sinful and incapable of turning our lives around without giving up our independence and free will, confessing our sins, and leaving our fate in the hands of God, AA or preferably both.

So you have a choice, either become an unquestioning sheep or an evolving member of the human species. Bah, you can take the easy path, or you can do the work and become what you are capable of!!!!

Chapter 8

AA almost gets it right

Steps 8-10 pretty much all relate to the same idea so I'll just list them here and then make a comment or two.

STEP 8- "Made a list of all persons we had harmed, and became willing to make amends to them all".

STEP 9- "Made direct amends to such people wherever possible, except when to do so would injure them or others."

STEP 10- "Continued to take personal inventory and when we were wrong promptly admitted it."

It's hard to argue with any of these premises. Admitting when you are wrong and trying to make things right are obviously a mature way of approaching life. It also makes sense to evaluate what is presently going on in your world and to make adjustments when appropriate. It comes down to doing the next right thing!

STEP 11- "Sought through prayer and meditation to improve our conscious contact with God *as we understood Him*, praying only for knowledge of His will for us and the power to carry that out."

This one is a bit tricky because it lumps prayer, meditation and God all together. Meditation can be religious or secular. Obviously Bill leans towards the Christian definition which deals with revelations towards God as opposed to secular meditation which is more about relaxation and self-awareness. The number of definitions and ways in which to go about meditation varies as widely as the number of religions that advocate its use in some form or another. At the end of the day, Step 11 is just the final declarative statement of AA's 12 step religion, reinforcing the idea that God will release you from your addiction if you ask Him to.

STEP 12- "Having had a spiritual awakening as the result of these steps, we tried to carry this message to alcoholics, and to practice these principles in all our affairs."

Mercifully we have arrived at AA's final step which on the face of it is an altruistic enough endeavor. Giving something back to those less fortunate than ourselves is one the greatest gifts that we can bestow upon others. While the intent of AA is for the most part is pure, there is an ulterior motive lurking behind this step as well. Like any other religious organization, one of its primary goals is to not only survive but to grow and make converts of non-believers. Back when Bill Wilson first founded AA, the primary method of growing the organization was by having active members seek out new ones.

This recruitment method has, for the most part, been rendered unnecessary. This is due to the fact that addiction specialists, rehabilitation facilities, hospital outpatient services, the legal system, and the media, have unfortunately done a very thorough job of promoting the notion that AA is the only viable resource for the suffering alcoholic. That being said, AA still uses this premise for the purpose of keeping one from ever leaving the flock. They see it as a member's responsibility to stay around to help guide the newcomers. Do not feel guilty about leaving!!!!! Besides the aforementioned methods of recruitment, there are enough "old timers" whose entire lives revolve around AA and who very happily take on this role.

We have finally exhausted our discussion regarding the 12 Steps and you are probably as tired of reading about them as I am of writing about them. If I have succeeded in my intent, then you have garnered some usable and constructive ideas. At the same time, you have hopefully concluded that to live your life using the 12 Step religion as a blueprint for life is less than desirable.

Chapter 9

The bane of AA existence-AA meetings

There are all kinds of AA meetings but by far the two most common are what's known as speaker and discussion meetings.

Speaker meetings are those in which a member of the group or a guest speaker discusses his history with regards to alcohol abuse. They share their "experience, strength and hope", by following the guidelines from the big book (page 58) which states; "Our stories disclose in a general way what we used to be like, what happened, and what we are like now." As mentioned previously, the first few pages of this "How it Works" chapter are often read by one of the members at the beginning of the meeting and this section also includes the 12 steps and "three pertinent ideas" (page 60):

"That we were alcoholic and could not manage our own lives."

"That probably no human power could have relieved our alcoholism."

"That God could and would if He were sought."

Discussion meetings are those where the facilitator introduces a subject and then shares some of his or her own views. In both of these types of gatherings, the meeting is then opened up to the floor and any member can share his or her opinion by raising their hand and being called on. General protocol dictates that members only share once during a meeting so as to avoid what is known as "cross talk". Essentially the idea is to not offer your personal opinions on what someone else has just said, interrupting someone's share or speaking out of turn. It is permissible to expand on the thoughts or ideas that somebody else has shared as long you are only expressing your experience and do not make it personal as in; "You're wrong John, this is the way it is".

To actually identify an AA meeting as a discussion meeting is completely erroneous because actual back and forth conversations are basically forbidden. This is a very convenient and calculated way for the facilitator to maintain control of the meeting while keeping any kind of critical or differing views of AA doctrine to a minimum. The facilitator simply thanks that person for their "share" and moves the meeting along. In other words, thanks for your blasphemous opinion; we will now move on to more constructive comments. If you actually have the guts to voice a highly critical thought, the facilitator will actually, in most cases, stop you in your tracks by saying something along the lines of; "Thanks Rolf, we have other people that need to share tonight." The end result of this is that most people's comments are either directed towards their abhorrent behavior when they were still active drinkers or they go on and on about how fantastic and wonderful their lives are now that they are part of the AA community. For the diehard member, these meetings, taking on the role of being a sponsor, and participating in other AA related activities consumes the vast majority of their free time. Honestly, it's kind of obsessive and bizarre.

The anatomy of a meeting

Most beginner meetings are a combination of speaker/discussion meetings in that after some opening formalities, someone begins the meeting by sharing his story and then the meeting is opened up into the "share" format.

I'm going to describe one of these meetings from the perspective of someone who is attending one for the first time so that you can get a sense of what that feels and looks like. AA groups, ironically, hold most of their meetings in church basements or meeting rooms. They meet at the same time each week, usually in the evening between 7:00PM and 8:00PM. There are, of course, meetings to be found at all hours of the day, but these are the most common times.

At the first meeting I ever attended, I sat in the parking lot of the church before the meeting just observing the arrival of the other attendees. There are usually a handful of people milling around outside smoking cigarettes or just socializing. Like most first timers that I've spoken to, I timed my entrance to pretty much coincide with the beginning of the meeting. It takes a lot of guts to walk into an AA meeting for the first time and feelings of fear, uncertainty, and self-loathing are usually just some of the emotions that are running through one's head at this time.

In many cases, upon entering the meeting room there will be a "greeter" who simply offers their hand and says "welcome". Ordinarily the room is set up with a small table in front and then rows of folding chairs for the congregation. Seated at the table are usually a facilitator and that day's speaker. The facilitator is a confirmed member of the group that has taken on the responsibility of taking on that role for a set period of time.

The culture shock of attending your first meeting

At my first meeting I had to make the decision of either hiding as far away in the back row as possible or to sit by the nearest exit so that I could make a quick escape. I am sure that I am by no means the first or last person to have taken on this strategy. In some meetings, you go around the room and everybody introduces themselves saying; "I'm Rolf and I'm an alcoholic", or just "Pete, alcoholic, Sue, alcoholic/addict", etc. I find this practice to be both demeaning and unnecessary. It has been pointed out to me that it is important for people to affirm their powerlessness and alcoholic condition. Honestly, if I'm sitting in a church basement at 8:00PM on a Monday night with a bunch of recovering alcoholics, it's pretty safe to assume that I am aware of the fact that I have a problem! Do I really have to partake in this demeaning admission every time I speak as some form of validation? You might as well just say, "Hi, I've been bad but I'm here to take my medicine". ACK, run away!!!!! I can only imagine how many people ran for the hills and never gave the program another look because of this annoying "confession" that is "suggested" of them. Even if I'm still on the fence as to whether I am or am not indeed an alcoholic, making me say that I am is not going to alter my opinion. I should state here, as I am sure that any devoted AA member would be quick to add, that AA has no rules or laws but that these traditions are mere "suggestions". In the hundreds of meetings that I've attended covering three separate states, I've only witnessed a handful of people who offer any kind of introduction other than those stated above. At the last few meetings I attended, I used the line; "Hi, I'm Rolf, I'm a recovered alcoholic and want to stay that way." As was expected, this introduction was met with the rolling of eyes and looks of sympathy. Over the years I learned that if you want to be a part of the "gang", you simply do not alter or question any kind of meeting protocol!

Along with the reading of "How it works", there are other rituals that usually take place at the beginning of a meeting. None of these are written in stone and each individual group is free to include whatever their group consciousness decides.

Either right before or after "How it works", the AA preamble is also cited as follows;

"Alcoholics Anonymous is a fellowship of men and women who share their experience, strength and hope with each other that they may solve their common problem and help others to recover from alcoholism. The only requirement for membership is a desire to stop drinking. There are no dues or fees for A.A. membership; we are self-supporting through our own contributions. A.A. is not allied with any sect, denomination, politics, organization or institution; does not wish to engage in any controversy, neither endorses nor opposes any causes. Our primary purpose is to stay sober and help other alcoholics to achieve sobriety."

Also very popular at meetings is the recital of what has become known as "The Promises" from pages 83-84 of the Big Book which goes as follows;

"If we are painstaking about this phase of our development, we will be amazed before we are half way through. We are going to know a new freedom and a new happiness. We will not regret the past nor wish to shut the door on it. We will comprehend the word serenity and we will know peace. No matter how far down the scale we have gone, we will see how our experience can benefit others. That feeling of uselessness and self-pity will disappear. We will lose interest in selfish things and gain interest in our fellows. Self-seeking will slip away. Our whole attitude and outlook upon life will change. Fear of people and of economic insecurity will leave us. We will intuitively know how to handle situations which used to baffle us. We will suddenly realize that God is doing for us what we could not do for ourselves. Are these extravagant promises? We think not. They are being fulfilled among us—sometimes quickly, sometimes slowly. They will always materialize if we work for them."

Let me state just a few observations about this passage. As far as not shutting the door on the past, I agree that we must take a look at what got us to this moment in time. For it is in the past that we have to discover what the underlying causes or events were that kept us from being happy with who and where we were. There are plenty of things in my past that I regret but I don't dwell on them. I use them as the learning experiences that they were meant to be and then move on. The problem with AA is that it is their belief that we have to forever rehash all of the terrible things we did during our addictive period otherwise we will "forget" all about them. Believe me, as most former addicts would most assuredly confirm, there are a plethora of things to remind us of that period of our lives without constantly having to go to meetings in church basements!

Along with the "three pertinent ideas" listed above, this paragraph once again emphasizes that the reason we are making progress is because God is doing it for us. Granted that a few sentences later Bill does admit that we have to work for it. As I've stated before, the Big Book contradicts itself continuously.

Perhaps the most awkward and disturbing moment of one's first meeting occurs right after when whomever is reading the passage gets to the part where they ask; "Are these extravagant promises?" The whole congregation then very enthusiastically and loudly answers in unison; *we think not!* It's extremely creepy and borderline cult-like.

Ok, time to get back to the meeting. It is usually at about this time when the facilitator will ask if there is anybody there for the first time, coming back or visiting from out of town who would like to introduce themselves. Again it is only a suggestion and one is not obligated to do so. All of the old-timers can spot a newcomer a mile away and while they will certainly give you a gander, it's certainly not meant to be done in a threatening or intimidating manner. I'm pretty sure that at my first meeting I tried my best to impersonate a ghost and did not raise my hand.

Again, the sequence of events varies, but usually at around this point the facilitator will remind those in attendance of the anonymous nature of AA by saying something along the lines of; "In the spirit of AA's tradition of anonymity, who you see here and what you hear here, should stay here".

Finally, a secretary's and treasurer's report may or may not be read and if anybody has any AA related announcements they can express them at this time. In some groups, these elements are brought up at the end of the meeting.

At most beginner meetings before introducing the evening's speaker, the facilitator will offer the following three suggestions to all newcomers.

    1-Join a home group

    2-Attend 90 meetings in 90 days

    3- Get a sponsor (men with the men, women with the women)

Yawn (Story time)

After all this, the speaker finally gets his opportunity to tell his or her story. I feel that it's important to include a story here because it will help to give you a feel for the flow of a meeting and to kind of bring home the point that listening to these every time you go to a meeting can become old pretty fast. In order to kill two birds with one stone, I will give you a brief rendition of my story. At least I'll use my example for the parts about "what we used to be like and what happened. As for the parts about what happened in terms of recovery and what we are like now, I'll give some generic examples being that I can't credit AA with that part of "my story". Everybody's tale and more importantly their underlying issues are all different and that is just one of the reasons why I feel that a generic recovery program like AA falls short in some vital areas. If you find yourself bored to tears, by all means skip ahead. Even enthusiastic AA members refer to these monologs as "drunkalogs".

Many of you when hearing my story may reasonably conclude that I had absolutely no reason whatsoever to have developed the debilitating condition of alcoholism. After all, neither of my parents drank alcoholically and I was raised in an upper middle if not lower upper class environment. There was no abuse of any kind to be found anywhere in my background.

Let me give you a quick history of my life before I had ever taken that first drink. I was born in Hannover, Germany in the summer of 1961 and my family moved from a small countryside village to New York City just prior to my third birthday. This was due to the fact that my father had landed an offer for a once in a lifetime business opportunity. To say that this was a culture shock for both my parents and my older brother would be a huge understatement. For me, not so much being that I was still a toddler.

Within a year, my father moved us out to the suburbs much to the relief of my mother and we were poised to start living the American dream. As a result of my young age when we arrived, I was the only one in the family that grew up gravitating towards typically American cultural institutions including such things as baseball, hot dogs, and Hot Wheels. I still lovingly remember my Dad watching a baseball game with me for about five minutes and observing that they all appeared to be; "older fat guys wearing pajamas who very sporadically chased around a little white ball!" It was the kind of take that a space alien might have, and in hindsight, if I were to be completely objective here, not far off the mark. The point being, that while my older brother was into soccer and took a keen interest in my father's engineering career, I was already forging my identity as the somewhat odd or different one of the bunch. Not that this had any bearing on my subsequent alcoholism but I think that these kinds of things help shape who and what you become and that it's important to go back and look at all of these things when you are trying to understand your makeup.

As a little boy and pre-teen I was extremely shy, self-conscious and had a slight developmental problem with my speech. This was no doubt partially the result of my having been born approximately six weeks premature.

By the time Junior High School rolled around, I was twelve years old but looked more like that of a nine or ten year old. Needless to say this only added to my anxiety as a youth. Like so many an alcoholic before and since, my first experience with booze provided instant relief. Anxiety immediately was replaced by confidence and a quiet meek disposition by an unbridled exuberance.

Looking back on that first drunk New Year's Eve close to forty years ago, I can see that I must have been constructed differently neurologically and genetically. The two neighborhood pals who joined me in stealing and sneaking drinks that night were also experiencing the alcohol high for the first time. Somewhere throughout that night they both wound up throwing up all over themselves and proceeded to wake up the following morning feeling like death warmed over. The idea of drinking any time too soon for either of them was pretty much inconceivable. For me, it was the complete opposite. I might have had a slight headache or hangover but it was by no means debilitating. I woke up feeling on top of the world and already trying to figure out how and when I could experience that euphoria again. Basically, my future as an addictive personality was cemented right then and there. A rebel without a cause was born!

Not that anybody ever forced me to take that first drink and head off to the races, but I do sometimes wonder where in the world my parents were when I decided to choose that path. Granted, it was the early 70's and society's attitude towards these things was extremely more relaxed than it is today. For the most part, parents weren't nearly as involved in their children's lives as the soccer moms and dads of today who are so involved in every facet of their kid's lives that it borders on overkill. But still, just saying. Maybe they thought I'd grow out of it. At the end of the day it probably wouldn't have made much of a difference. If they had suddenly decided to turn into strict disciplinarians overnight, I would have just rebelled against that that much harder. I had made my decision and that was that.

The negative ramifications for my poor choices manifested in quick order. Instead of becoming involved in sports or excelling academically, I just floundered, hung out with the burn outs and found ways to find my booze, weed or anything else that I could get my hands on. My brother was a star athlete in track, soccer, etc. while also maintaining a 4.0 GPA and being voted most likely to succeed! To my parents' credit, they never gave me the "why can't you be more like your brother" speech. I just didn't care and that was pretty much my attitude for the rest of high school.

Even though I never cracked a book or studied for a test, I still managed to get good enough grades to get into college and thus continue the party. It took me five and a half years to graduate because of an incident that occurred my sophomore year. Some friends of mine had decided to visit from home unannounced and were accused of having committed a significant amount of vandalism on the campus. It turns out that they weren't the guilty party but with my reputation as a partier, the accusations somehow came my way. So once again my lifestyle was causing major problems in my life. I ended up transferring and finishing my education at a local college.

Not having any clue as to what I wanted to do with my life, I majored in business/marketing because I figured that I eventually would need to get a job in the business world. Not too much soul searching or logical reasoning went into that decision making process. Without a stellar GPA and no real direction in mind, my marketing degree led to a sales career that I found to be neither stimulating or rewarding, nor even remotely enjoyable. It never even occurred to me that I had choices.

Within two and half years I was married. Some people put forward the theory that you stop growing and maturing emotionally the moment you become addicted to any substance. I tend to agree with this sentiment and in my case that means that at this point in my life I was essentially a twelve year old living inside the body of a twenty six year old! Sure I thought I loved my wife, but did I even know what that meant? So time marched on and we had three fantastic children who were, as my ex-wife is often quick to point out, the only redeeming result of our union together. I can't really argue her position.

By the end of my drinking saga, I was consuming at least a quart of vodka a day around the clock. Once the seal of that puppy was cracked, it was a goner. There was no such thing as a two day old bottle!

It is said that you have to reach your "bottom" before you will be motivated to change. I kind of think that bottom means death, so you had better find a reason to alter your course before that. Obviously I hadn't sank that low but after losing my family, employment and the roof over my head in quick succession, I suppose I had come close enough to the cellar that something finally flicked the switch. I decided that I didn't want to die just yet.

I'll cover the non-AA recovery part of my story in a later chapter. For now, I'll give you a general idea of where most people in AA go when discussing this part of their journey. A typical progression might go something like this;

"It was when I came into these halls that my life was transformed. I immediately felt the hope and strength that all of you people were experiencing and I knew that I wanted that too. I listened to the suggestions in the meetings and as outlined in the big book. I got a sponsor and eventually did the steps with his/her guidance. Because of this program and you people, I now have a life second to none." Obviously that's the short version but these are pretty much the sentiments that are expressed. This part of the story telling is usually fairly brief because everybody usually more or less says the same thing with slight variations.

Time to share

As I mentioned, after the speaker has finished with his part, the meeting is opened up for sharing among the group. Beginners are given the opportunity to share first if they are so inclined. While they will sometimes relate to something the speaker has said and compare some part of their history to their own experience, more often than not, they will discuss what is going on with them personally at the present moment in terms of how they are dealing with their new found sobriety. The more tenured members are more inclined to chime in with statements like; "Thanks for sharing John, I can totally relate to that part of your story where you ... Like you, I am grateful for the new life that this program has given me..."

At the end of the meeting the facilitator will ask by the show of hands if there are any members of the group that are available to assume the role of temporary sponsors for any of the newcomers in attendance who may have an interest. Often times, these temporary sponsors will end up becoming permanent.

At last the meeting has come to an end and the group stands in a circle to hold hands and recite either the Lord's Prayer or the Serenity Prayer. Again, you can opt out of this ritual but very few do.

I will give a brief description of meetings that are based on AA literature (Big Book and 12 & 12) in a subsequent chapter. The third key component to the AA movement, besides the steps and meetings, involves that of the sponsor and that is what I will touch upon next.

Chapter 10

Be wary of sponsors!

As mentioned in the previous chapter, one of AA's primary "suggestions" for newcomers is that they choose a sponsor as soon as possible upon joining the fellowship. There are people within AA, however, who simply choose to attend meetings and have not embraced doing the steps and or utilizing the services of a sponsor. To be fair, if you sincerely want the program of AA to deliver what it proclaims to offer, you should probably follow these prompts.

A sponsor is simply a mentor or a guide, somebody from the AA group who will be there to support you as you make your way through the AA program. Ideally you will choose somebody who has done all of the steps themselves so that they can help you navigate through them for yourself. They should also be available to answer any questions that you may have regarding any of the ideas and concepts that you may encounter while reading the AA literature. It is further proposed that you work together when formulating and writing down your "moral inventory" for the fourth step. While it is not mandatory, as nothing in the program of AA supposedly is, more often than not, it is the sponsor that will be chosen to hear one's fifth step confession.

When having first established a relationship with your sponsor, it is suggested that you call or "check in" with him or her at least once a day. Ideally, your mentor is supposed to keep their advice limited to areas of growth in such areas as program knowledge and spirituality. Areas in which they are advised not to give advice include but are not limited to such subjects as personal finance, legal, marital and family issues. Unfortunately this ideal is rarely adhered to by both sponsors and sponsees alike. I've met far too many people who depend on their sponsors to make virtually every important decision in their life for them. This kind of dependence is unhealthy and inhibits personal growth instead of fostering it. In some cases they are so dependent on this relationship and support that they become somewhat unglued if they are out of contact for even a few short days.

Now don't get me wrong, there are a lot of very knowledgeable, compassionate and intuitive people who take on the selfless and helpful role of being a sponsor. On the flip side, however, there are also those that become sponsors because they are egomaniacs and enjoy the power that comes along with telling people what to do. The problem is that there is no real way of knowing, other than through observation at meetings, who would make a decent sponsor. The only qualification for being a sponsor is that one has to have accumulated at least one year of sobriety under their belt. That's it!!!!! At least a priest has to go through years of training to be qualified to hear one's confession in the church. Psychiatrists and other mental health professionals have to go through years of education in order to offer advice. In order to be an AA sponsor, there are no classes that need to be taken; no tests to pass or any kind of certification process whatsoever! I can't emphasize enough here how dangerous and irresponsible it is to put so much dependence on someone who has absolutely NO business nor qualifications for running your life and making life altering decisions for you.

From bad to worse

I can think of many disconcerting sponsor stories and I'll share just a few here while changing the names of those involved in order to protect their anonymity.

Tony, the wise one

Tony was one of those "old timers" who was highly respected throughout the entire local AA community. By his own admission he had up to as many as ten sponsees at any given time under his guidance. He was retired and so therefore had an endless supply of time in which to take on that role. It was at a discussion meeting one morning when he delivered a confession that would leave absolutely everybody in attendance speechless. He very nonchalantly informed everybody that he was celebrating his seventh day of sobriety and that he had fallen off the wagon sixteen months prior. Not only was he chairing meetings while drunk, he was also guiding a handful of sponsees the entire time! Talk about not walking the walk but talking the talk!

Joey, the kid

Joey was a really nice, polite and sincere young man who celebrated his first year of sobriety at the tender young age of 19. I'll never forget the look of excitement on his face when he gleefully raised his hand in order to volunteer for the position of temporary sponsor at his one year anniversary. I mean honestly, Joey is the first to admit that his life was a train wreck from the time he was 13 until he finally put the drugs and booze down at 18. He's just a kid that graduated from high school by the skin of his teeth. He barely has a grasp of who he is and certainly doesn't have the insight and wisdom from which to start trying to help someone else get their life together.

Don't tell me what to do

I've personally only attempted the sponsor thing on two short lived occasions. In one instance, I was having a really hard time dealing with the fact that I had lost my job and the bills were starting to mount up. It was while my sponsor was helping me with my fourth step laundry list that I confided in him exactly how much stress this was causing me. His advice on the matter was to forget about it, that my only concern at this time should to be to worry about staying sober "one day at a time". Easy for Charlie to say as he had 13 years of sobriety under his belt along with a thriving practice as a pediatrician. While I agree that job hunting and networking is extremely unpractical while you are still going through detoxification, once you are on the road to recovery you need to get back to being a responsible parent, spouse and member of society sooner than later. Many people who are new to AA also spend so much time at meetings and with their sponsor that they neglect their families. The idea that it is "OK" to immerse oneself so completely in the program particularly at the onset is also supported by passages in the Big Book. The mindset is that family, friends, and employers should be infinitely patient and supportive of the idea that their significant other needs to make AA priority number one. Obviously getting sober and staying that way should be a top priority but not at the expense of facing reality and your worldly obligations!

Steve's tragic and avoidable death

The last story that I will share here has such a tragic ending and still angers me to this day. Steve had been in the program for a few years but was still not finding a sense of contentment and purpose. He clearly still had unresolved issues which AA was unable to help him identify and address. His sponsor, Paul, a long time AA member with quite a few sponsees under his direction, cared greatly for Steve and did everything in his power to help him recover. Unfortunately everybody's best efforts and intentions just didn't take. Steve stopped going to meetings and calling Paul. At a loss as to what to do, he resumed his destructive drinking life. Several months later, Paul ran into Steve in town, at which time he broke down sobbing and told Paul that he felt that life was too much to bear; that he just couldn't do it anymore and that he wanted to die. Paul's advice to Steve was simply this; "Gee Steve, you stopped going to meetings and calling me, you know what you have to do. See you at the meeting tonight." Steve hung himself that night!

Yes, maybe if Steve had kept going to meetings and calling Paul every day he would still be here. He would have kept changing his AA bandage and been a functioning but miserable recovering alcoholic. The point is that for Steve, eking out sobriety one day at a time wasn't good enough. AA wasn't working for him and now he was lost. I didn't know Steve and maybe he had severe emotional and mental health issues that required professional help. The point is that Paul was not qualified to offer a "solution" to somebody who was threatening to take their own life. He should have called 911 or at the very least not left him out of his sight until he was speaking in a more calm rational tone and was sure that he was not in danger of harming himself. Paul still happily recounts this story as if to drive home the point that if you listen to your sponsor and do as he says, then all will be well in the world. Tell that to Steve's nine year old daughter!

Most sponsors mean well

Again to be fair, I must state again that most everybody that takes on the role of a sponsor does so for the reason of helping others. Many a sponsor will point out, however, that they too receive a huge benefit by doing so. Simply by freely giving of yourself towards the noble cause of helping another, you derive a sense of self-worth and value. An all too common trait of many an addict is that of selfishness and isolation. Extending yourself as a sponsor is a good way to help address both of those characteristics.

The problem here is that some people become sponsors

just because they think it will help keep them sober. They don't really care about their sponsees and only take on the role because the "old timers" convince them that to do so is their responsibility.

Just keep in mind that your sponsor is just another person that stopped drinking before you did and that has preferably completed his step work. Most alcoholics have also done a marvelous job of alienating many of their friends and acquaintances so adding a new one can't hurt either. So the advice here when considering asking somebody to be your sponsor is to choose carefully and to realize that they are in no way a professional therapist with any sort of formal training. With that in mind, consider their advice but weigh it against your own rational reasoning and don't simply accept their opinions as inarguable truths.

Chapter 11

AA's Bible study-oops-I mean literature based meetings

Along with speaker, discussion and beginner meetings, the two other major types of meetings are based on AA's two literary staples, The 12 & 12 (Twelve Steps and Twelve Traditions) and the Big Book (Alcoholics Anonymous).

Both meetings begin with the traditional announcements and are also facilitated by a moderator. In a Step meeting, one of the 12 steps is chosen as the topic for the evening based on whatever step was completed the week before. Seating is often arranged in a circle or around a large table so that each member can take a turn reading a paragraph or two from the chapter dedicated to that step.

At the end of the reading, the moderator will usually share his or her feelings on the subject and expand on how incorporating the different aspects of the step have helped them maintain their ongoing sobriety and spiritual connectedness. After the moderator has shared his or her thoughts, the meeting is opened up to the group to do the same. I feel that the reading of the steps takes too much time out of the meeting and it would be more useful if the members came in having already done so, so that they could get right into the analysis part. I suppose the reason for it being done that way is so anybody can walk in and know what's going on. Although I don't agree with most of the steps, at least in these meetings the dialog is more focused as opposed to just rehashing stories and having people comment on how wonderful the program is.

Big Book meetings are run primarily the same way, with a passage of the text selected by the moderator and an open discussion that follows. While there are many insightful and thought provoking ideas put forth in these pages, there is also in my opinion, an equally large amount of curious conclusions and faulty logic. Just because Mr. Wilson says so, doesn't make it so. The sad truth is, however, that the majority of people in AA do treat the writings and "suggestions" in the big book as dogma. Again, Bill had no formal education regarding religion, psychology or medicine. I'm not saying that one can't acquire a great deal of knowledge and understanding on any given subject by means of researching and learning for oneself. I'm just saying that to take everything that Mr. Wilson has to say as inarguable truths is doing yourself a disservice. I am, in fact, a huge supporter of the premise that through our own self-will and desire to grow and evolve, that we have an endless capacity to change and create a more meaningful and healthy reality for ourselves.

Therein lays the fundamental difference between AA and my evolutionary view of recovery. AA believes that you are powerless and that in order to overcome your addiction that you must abdicate your free will and put all of your hope and dreams of recovery into the guidance of someone or something else. I propose that the higher power that is needed resides within the individual. It's just a matter of developing that well of potential. Is it easy? Hell no; it requires desire, education, responsibility, change and a lot of incredibly hard work. The alternative is to be a sheep in constant need of a new AA bandage.

You are not a sheep so let's get to work, evolve and beat this thing once and for all!

Chapter 12

AA Member Survey

In order to give the AA community a voice and an opportunity to make a case for the organization's effectiveness, I created a survey towards that end and found that the results further reinforced my conclusion that AA's "program" is extreme and at times unhealthy. Getting individuals to participate was difficult, as the AA community is very guarded, suspicious and protective of their flock. In order to protect people's identities, I am using only fictitious names and backgrounds as I personally know some of the respondents.

The range of participation runs the gamut from casual to extreme. On the mild to moderate side I will share "Kenny's" and "Lisa's" views and involvement in the program.

Kenny told me that he got sober in AA nine years ago and that he attends meetings maybe once a month on average. When he first started, he went maybe twice a week and found the support of others who shared his struggle to be both comforting and constructive. He never sought out a sponsor and said that he really didn't immerse himself in the 12 steps. For him, just being able to vent about his struggles and to hear some useful advice was enough for him. He says that he still goes because he made some good friends there and that the occasional meeting helps keep him grounded. It's a good reminder of where he came from and doesn't want to return to. This "reminder" aspect is one of AA's major selling points and some people take it way too far as an "essential" part of recovery.

Lisa's involvement is fairly "typical" of those who find

AA to be an integral part of their "ongoing" recovery and I will share her responses in their entirety.

How long have you been attending AA?

"I'll have 6 years on March 14th"

How many meetings a week to you go to? Why?

"1 or 2 depending on the week. I go to get my medicine and to stay right sized."

"Right sized" is one of dozens of AA slogans that members can't help but have hammered into their brains if they go to enough meetings. When I asked Lisa what she meant by that she replied; "If I don't go to enough meetings, I start getting all full of myself. Like I'm OK on my own."

What does AA mean to you? How important is it your life? Why? What is it about AA that works for you?

"AA is extremely important to me. It's what keeps me going. The people in the rooms get me. It gives me structure and a sense of belonging. I really can't imagine my life without it."

Have you ever slipped since you've been in the program? Why do you think it happened? Was it hard for you to come back?

"Oh, God yes! I think I slipped about 4 times in the first half year. It was always the same thing. I wasn't going to enough meetings or calling my sponsor. Everybody knows that once you start doing that, that you are bound to fall. I'll never let that happen again. The first time I was ashamed and afraid to come back. But the people here don't judge you and always welcome you back."

This is one of AA's greatest myths. That God forbid you leave the program, it's virtually guaranteed that you will be back to drinking alcoholically in short order. That is simply untrue.

Did you enjoy your first AA meeting? What were your impressions or feelings?

"Are you kidding me? I was terrified! Everybody there looked so damned happy and it pissed me off. At the same time, I wished I felt that way so I came back."

Do you have a sponsor? How often do you call or see them? Do you ask them for advice and guidance on non-alcohol related issues? Why? What makes you believe they are qualified to offer you advice on such issues?

"Peggy has been my sponsor since the very beginning; she's awesome. She has so much insight and wisdom. I see her at almost every meeting and I call her all the time. She has over 20 years! Why would I even think of questioning her advice?"

As I mentioned in my chapter on sponsors (chapter 10), there are absolutely NO requirements in order to become a sponsor other than having at least one year of sobriety. The idea that someone without any professional training or accreditation whatsoever is depended on to give life altering advice is absolutely frightening. Don't get me wrong, there are some very compassionate, intelligent and sincere people who take on this role. At the same time, there are also many egotistical, ignorant and selfish people who seem to love the role of telling people what to do and how to live their lives!

Do you have a higher power and if so, what is it?

"I do! Well I've always believed in God but now I have something more to hold onto."

What do you mean?

"I don't know. Somehow being in AA, following the steps, it all makes me feel connected."

Most people, when asked, will say that they have a higher power of their own understanding, whatever that means. This is another pat answer that is supplied through the AA litera- ture. A few, however, will honestly readily admit that the institution of AA itself IS their higher power.

What does "One day at a time" mean to you? How do you apply it to your life?

"Just what it says. That by going to meetings, reading the big book and calling my sponsor, that I can stay sober one day at a time. You know, just for today."

And then you do that again the next day and then the next, etc.?

"Well yeah, that's how it works."

Have you worked the steps? If so, what did the experience do for you?

"Several times! I learn more about myself each time. It's kind of like my roadmap for life."

I'm sorry but I think that a "roadmap" that instructs you to give up your free will, confess your sins to free yourself of guilt and to declare yourself as powerless without the fellowship of AA to guide you, is hardly one that you should embrace. Unless of course, that is all you as an individual are capable of.

How was step 4 (Made a searching and fearless moral inventory of ourselves) useful?

"It made me look at all the crappy shit that I did."

And this was helpful how?

"You have to take ownership of that stuff and make it right if you can".

While I can't really argue with this idea, what bothers me is that AA encourages you to revisit this step all the time. It does that by "suggesting" that you share your "story" in meetings and also suggests that one never really stop doing the steps. There are even "step meetings" in which you can revisit these steps ad nauseam. It's "one day at a time" all over again. Yes, history can repeat itself if you don't learn from it. So learn from it and move on for crying out loud!

Step 5 (*Admitted to God, to ourselves, and to another human being the nature of our wrongs*) How did this confession step of AA help you? Do you feel that by having gone through this step that the burdens of your past have been removed?

"It's coming clean, admitting you fucked up. Yeah, I admitted my shit, made my apologies. I'm good!"

Whether or not confession absolves you of your past misdeeds is clearly an idea that is open for debate. Personally I don't think so. Just ask the people that you've hurt if your confession really changes anything. If they are kind and for-giving they will give you a pass anyway but your confession doesn't achieve anything other than making you feel better about your role in it all.

How does your family feel about the extent to which you are involved with the program?

"The kids are young so they don't really know much. Thank God! My husband, Eric, thinks that it's weird and a bit over the top but I'm not drinking so he's basically OK with it."

Do you think that you are still "powerless" over alcohol? Why?

"Hell yes! Left to my own devices, I'd be screwed."

If you stopped going to meetings or left AA, do you think that you would drink again?

"No doubt about it, I wouldn't have my support system. I'd forget where I came from."

If you hang around AA long enough, you will hear that dire prediction time and time again.

Do you feel that you had any underlying issues that led to your drinking? Have you figured out what they were and if so, what were they and how did you figure them out? Are they now resolved? If so, why do you feel that you still need the program?

"Who knows, I just know that I was a train wreck when I got here and now my life is better than ever thanks to my friends, my sponsor and the program."

Practically nobody that I interviewed identified any particular problem areas in their life that they have resolved as a result of their association with Alcoholics Anonymous. Is it any wonder then that AA doesn't last or work for so many folks? Most people, after varying amounts of time, just don't want to eke out life "one day at a time".

How do you feel about AA literature? (The Big Book and the 12 & 12)

"It's gotten millions of people sober and helps keep them that way so I'm sold!"

The extent to which members of AA hang onto and believe in every word ever written by Bill Wilson is truly astounding.

Do you think that there is any value in any "non-AA approved" ideas or literature?

"I suppose, don't really know because I get everything I need right here."

If you ever try and bring up alternative ideas about recovery at a meeting or even while conversing with folks before or after a meeting, you will be met with cold glares and even more annoyingly, with condescension. AA has no room or tolerance for non-believers! They won't throw you out but you'll wish that they had.

Is there anything about AA that bothers you or that you don't like?

"Like with any other group, it can get a bit clicky but I don't worry or deal with that. I've got my friends and that's good enough for me."

Do you have any final thoughts on the fellowship?

"I'm grateful; I don't know where I'd be without it".

So all in all, Lisa seems like she is a fairly happy, grateful and content person and credits it all to AA. That's all good and if it works for her, there is nothing wrong with that on the face of it. That being said, I'll bet that if she were to decide to stop going to meetings she would discover that the world would not end and that she would be just fine. The problem is that for every Lisa that is thrilled to be a member of AA, there are many, many more Lisa's who try AA and don't get that warm and fuzzy feeling. As a result, they might actually believe that there is something wrong with them because they don't get it. I'm sure a lot of them finally do recover on their own. The tragedy lies in the fact that many of them won't.

I won't bore you with word for word answers from the fanatics that attend 8-10 meetings a week, believe that Bill Wilson was some kind of a prophet, fear for their sobriety if they don't talk to their sponsor daily, etc.. The sad truth is that this type of devotion is not rare in the least.

Though I no longer consider myself to be an active member of AA, I will share with you how I would answer the questions posed.

How long have you been attending AA?

"I am no longer an active member of AA but was involved with the program on five separate durations of varying lengths. The first time was when I was court ordered to attend at the age of 36 after I had been arrested for Driving Under the Influence (DUI). At that time I knew that I was becoming increasingly more dependent on alcohol to face the stresses of everyday life, but I was not ready to admit to myself or any-body else for that matter, that I was indeed an alcoholic.

On two subsequent occasions I became involved after

having completed two separate 30 day in-patient rehabilitation programs. Almost all of these facilities insist that attendance of AA is a "must" if you are to have any chance of lasting sobriety. Putting my trust with the experts after having spent large sums of money on my recovery, I listened and did as I was told.

My last foray into the program doesn't really count because I was attending strictly for research purposes for this book. Attending from the outside looking in was extremely enlightening in terms of really witnessing the effects of the program on newcomers and old-timers alike.

How many meetings a week do you go to? Why?

When I was attending AA regularly I went to 1 or 2 meetings a week. On one occasion, I actually did attend the suggested ninety meetings in the first ninety days. I'm sorry but that was one of the most painful three months that I've ever endured! I tried to have an open mind and have a good attitude, but I simply hated it and found it so repetitive that it bored me to tears.

What does AA mean to you? How important is it in your life? Why? What is it about AA that works for you?

Obviously AA did not work for me. Having to accept the idea that I was powerless, to identify myself as an alcoholic every time that I spoke, the thought of turning my WILL and my LIFE over to some higher power of my own choosing, and the AA premise that you must attend for life in order to maintain your sobriety, was absolutely unacceptable!

Have you ever slipped since you've been in the program? Why do you think it happened? Was it hard for you to come back?

I slipped every time I was in the program because it didn't address any of my underlying issues. Yes, during every attempt my attendance waned and I did indeed go back to drinking. Had I continued to go every day, eat, breathe and wholeheartedly embrace the process, I probably would have remained sober but still been miserable because my problems would not have gone away. I ripped off the AA bandage because I knew in my heart that I could not live that way for the rest of my life.

Did you enjoy your first AA meeting? What were your impressions or feelings?

No, I couldn't stand it. It felt like a religious cult. I'm not saying that AA is a cult because it clearly is not, but it sure felt like one and it does share some of the classic characteristics of one.

Do you have a sponsor? How often do you call or see them? Do you ask them for advice and guidance on non-alcohol related issues? Why? What makes you think they are qualified to offer you advice on such issues?

I only attempted the sponsor thing twice and I covered that on my chapter regarding the subject. I'll just say here that I was not comfortable with the whole concept. Again, there are virtually no qualifications for becoming a sponsor and I just couldn't turn over the direction of my life to somebody whose only claim to enlightenment was one plus year of sobriety! Picking a "bad" sponsor could be one of the most damaging things that a person could do.

Do you have a higher power and if so, what is it?

As I previously stated, I do not claim any kind of formal religious affiliation but do consider myself to be a spiritual person. I believe in "something" but prefer not to put a label on it because I don't think it's that simple.

What does "One day at a time" mean to you? How do you apply it to your life?

Ideally this should be a call to live in the present and that's what most people in AA claim it to be. In AA practice, however, members are continually reliving their painful past by telling their stories, being self-critical and forever labeling themselves as alcoholics. You are expected to surrender your will and life as opposed to determining your own reality. This leads one to fear losing their "present" sobriety unless they embrace AA's "suggestions" for eternity. "One day at a time" living instills guilt and fear instead of fostering personal growth and freedom.

Have you worked the steps? If so, what did the experience do for you?

Honestly I found that the process further enhanced my feelings of having failed at life. The whole thing is aimed at re-enforcing the notion that salvation can only be achieved by being a life-long AA 12 stepper.

How was step 4 (Made a searching and fearless moral inventory of ourselves) useful?

I have to admit that doing this step made me take a look at the destructive consequences of my alcoholic life. That being said, it did not necessarily help me uncover any of my underlying issues that led me to that way of living.

Step 5 (Admitted to God, to ourselves, and to another human being the nature of our wrongs) How did this confession step of AA help you? Do you feel that by having gone through this step that the burdens of your past have been removed?

No! Confession is nothing but a simple and inauthentic way to try and shirk your responsibility. Simply admitting that you screwed up and saying you're sorry, achieves very little.

How does your family feel about the extent to which you are involved with the program?

My family was desperate and believed the myth that AA was the only solution. Even though it felt wrong from the very beginning, I believed it too and attempted to "work" the program on more occasions and for longer durations than my intuition told me I should. This was a direct result of my desire to make them happy.

Do you think that you are still "powerless" over alcohol? Why?

Obviously not! If you haven't figured that one out by now, then I have failed miserably in the writing of this book. I know that I can't drink again but that hardly makes me powerless.

If you stopped going to meetings or left AA, do you think that you would drink again?

I believed that lie for far too long! Can I guarantee that I will never drink again? I don't think that anybody can ever really do that. Do I think that I will? Not in a million years. I absolutely love my second chance at life and have no intentions of testing those waters again. I've been there, done that and the results were not pretty.

Do you feel that you had any underlying issues that led to your drinking? Have you figured out what they were and if so, what were they and how did you figure them out? Are they now resolved? If so, why do you feel that you still need the program?

Absolutely!!!! Everybody has their own unique issues so listing mine isn't that important. Yes, I looked at my life's history but instead of berating myself for what I did wrong, I concentrated on trying to understand why. More importantly, I made a commitment to change, learn and evolve. I read about addiction, philosophy, recovery, psychology, religion and more. It is a lifelong process that is both fun and enlightening.

How do you feel about AA literature? (The Big Book & the 12 & 12)

While there are some valid and useful ideas put forth in both of these works, I find the logic and foundation to be faulty and at times downright dangerous. What really boggles my mind is that the AA faithful take every word ever written by Bill Wilson to be the truth and nothing but the truth. Other than being an alcoholic, he had no background in anything. Get as much information from as many resources as possible and discover your own truth and create your own reality.

Do you think that there is any value in any "non-AA approved" ideas or literature?

I certainly hope that you the reader will think so! See the above answer. So much of life lies in one's intent. It is my intent to offer a healthy and constructive alternative to the way in which the miserable condition of alcoholism is both viewed and addressed.

Is there anything about AA that bothers you or that you don't like?

I think that I pretty much covered this territory. Again, if you truly believe that being a member of AA and adhering to their lifelong program is the only way by which you can remain sober, then by all means, please stay. Being an AA sheep is better than being a hopeless drunk.

Do you have any final thoughts on the fellowship?

AA is extremely static and resistant to change so it really is pointless to list ways in which I think it could become more useful. I simply don't accept its two major premises that; 1- We are powerless and 2-That only a "higher power" can help one recover. There are other "support" groups out there that don't have a religious base but I really don't know enough about them to offer an opinion. The fellowship is a bandage that works but with a price tag that rips away your individuality, hope and joy. You lose hope because AA preaches that the best that you can ever achieve is to become a "recovering" alcoholic. As far as I'm concerned, if you no longer drink then you are no longer an alcoholic and you have recovered. You lose your individuality and joy because living an AA life is like being a "deer in the headlights" with a "Stepford Wives" kind of bliss. I honestly believe that living this way amounts to settling for survival instead of embracing the possible.

Part two of the book will explore these possibilities and much, much more.

Part Two

"Dress for success"
How to happily determine and fulfill
your life's potential and direction through the use
of evolved thinking and free-will

Chapter 13

Why me? How did I get here?

The AMA (American Medical Association) has classified alcoholism as a disease. AA pioneers called it an allergy. My only real argument against either idea is the fact that it is self-inflicted. No, you don't become an addict on purpose, but you do in fact, do it to yourself. Whatever it is or exactly how and why it manifests itself in certain people is still widely debated. The point is that at the end of the day, for you anyway, it really doesn't matter does it?

For those of you out there who don't believe that you have any underlying issues whatsoever and just don't understand why **you** of all people should be addicted to alcohol, the answer is quite simple. Because you are! You are wired differently and have crossed a line that you can't undo. If you are truly in the extreme minority of alcoholics who have suffered very little or no psychological or behavioral ramifications from your drinking other than getting in trouble with loved ones or employers, then your only solution is fairly clear. ACCEPT it and stop. Before you so quickly lump yourself into this category, however, consider the following scenario and see if you find yourself hiding somewhere in there.

You were just a confident person who drank with the guys and gals because it was fun. You might argue that there were no problems, so why did you become an alcoholic? Because even for you, eventually the big party stops being fun. The neurochemical changes that occur in your brain as a result of prolonged abuse accelerate as you keep drinking large quantities of alcohol consistently. For you, it may have started with the actual physical addiction itself with only a minimum of mental baggage. But that baggage will increase because addiction will eventually take a confident, morally good and socially conscious person and slowly turn them into a selfish, arrogant, and uncaring human being. Friends will start to fade because all you start to care about is yourself and chasing the high. Hobbies will disappear, striving for excellence will start to wane, and having an interest in your fellow man becomes less important. Apathy becomes your normal state of being. Maintaining healthy relationships starts becoming a chore. Does any of this resonate with you?

Regardless of what age you are when you begin to drink alcoholically, from that moment forward your ability to develop or even maintain healthy mature relationships goes into the toilet. The bottle increasingly becomes your most important companion and slowly but surely everybody else is left behind. Making matters even worse, your tolerance for anybody or anything that gets in the way of this love affair with your addiction becomes practically non-existent. Your ability to deal with life's stresses and setbacks deteriorates to the point where you stop even trying and just seek out your bottle buddy. All sense of empathy towards other people and their needs become alien because at this point it's all about you!

Another reason why we lose our ability to enjoy life is due to the biochemical and medical ramifications of drinking alcoholically. There is evidence to suggest that addiction/alcoholism causes permanent changes to one's brain chemistry. Prolonged and excessive alcohol consumption depletes some of the neurotransmitters in the brain. For example, Dopamine depletion can leave a person with a high tolerance to pain and a reduced level of the pleasure one feels when doing an activity. Serotonin depletion can lead to sensory deprivation, body temperature anomalies, and also depression. One's memory is also adversely affected by years of alcohol abuse. Fortunately, over time these things tend to improve immensely but one has to be patient, which goes against many alcoholics' nature.

For those of you that are willing to admit that there might be other underlying issues at play, or that maybe your life coping skills are possibly lacking to some degree, then the chapters that follow will help you to learn how to evolve into a sober and unique person who has the ability to embrace life and its potential. If your life skills were in pretty good shape before your alcoholism took root, then your path back to sound mental health should be less arduous than for those who never really developed them. In either case, you have work to do.

Alcoholism is a progressive condition that virtually nobody in their right mind chooses. Maybe that's the point. Within the minds of those afflicted, something is not right. Genetics, family history and life circumstances all contribute, but the bottom line again is that once you've crossed the line, you no longer have a choice as far as to whether or not you can drink like everybody else. In a sense, the only other choice that you ever really had was to never pick up a drink in the first place. Very few people make that choice because they aren't aware of their brain's "differentness" concerning alcohol. There are many in the medical field in agreement that a certain percentage of the population is blessed with the potential or brain chemistry to become an alcoholic. Congratulations! You're special. You're one of them but it's not your fault! The universe, higher power or whatever, decided that you would be born with that lovely potential to be part of the club. Now that doesn't mean that you will be, but you are in the lucky select class that is considered for enrollment.

So, if we only have the potential, why do we become addicted in the first place? I believe that alcoholism is not so much a disease as it is a symptom of something much deeper than that.

If by nature, you are anxious, nervous, shy, etc..., your chances of being in the graduating class go way up. You start to drink to alleviate pain and suffering. Something undefined is missing and you don't feel whole. Drinking puts you into a euphoric state that alleviates the constant dysfunction of your daily existence. Alcohol works for a while but the truly evil thing about it is that it will eventually leave you more anxious, stressed and isolated than you were before you ever picked up that first drink. You are seeking meaning, purpose and contentment in your life but the end result is that alcohol will provide you with exactly the opposite.

There are also many people who suffered from horrific mental and or physical abuse in their pre-addictive life. It's quite understandable that folks who have lived through this kind of trauma will do anything to alleviate the pain and anguish that comes as part of that experience.

Alcoholism is toxic to your soul! It robs and depletes you of all of your hope, joy, passion, interest, and ambition. It causes you to isolate yourself and withdraw from life. All that is left is the pursuit of oblivion.

You're not a bad person!

Again, the good news is the fact that the reason you've become an alcoholic is not entirely your fault. The bad news is that it's happened and it is your responsibility and yours alone to fix it. Actually this isn't really such bad news because once you accept this premise; the opportunities to create both a positive meaning and purpose to your life are endless!

While I will soon be addressing how vitally important decision making is in your life, I am going to ask you to make a huge decision this very moment and to stick to it. Decide to FORGIVE yourself for your addictive nature and the mess that it has caused. There was no malicious intent! This is probably one of the hardest things that you must do on the road to recovery but it is essential.

So much of life revolves around intent. Does anybody intentionally become addicted and alienate themselves from people and life? No, but that's what addiction does. You didn't wake up one day and decide that maybe becoming addicted and destroying your relationships with your family, your employer and the world in general was a good idea. Clearly that was never your intent or reason. You are not a bad or evil person. It just often happens to those with the predisposition towards alcoholism. Once addicted, all reason and intent pretty much fly off the radar.

The fact is that you have to just STOP. Well yeah, you might be saying to yourself, that's what needs to be done, but it's clearly not that easy. No, it's not easy but the most worthwhile and rewarding aspects of living rarely are and require effort, knowledge and skill.

How to do it then? If you are willing to expend the effort, then the tools necessary to accomplish anything you put your mind to are there for the taking.

You are not powerless!

AA believes that God will provide you with hope and purpose; that your higher power will alleviate all of your ills if you let it. I am by no means implying that spirituality or religion should not be a big part of your life. As previously mentioned I am quite spiritual in nature and believe in God, a universal intelligence or whatever you want to call it. Again, I prefer not to even put a name to it because for me that somehow diminishes it. There are so many fantastic ideals and concepts in all religions, ranging from the great monotheisms to Eastern religions, which instruct people to be kinder, more compassionate, forgiving, etc.

My point is that you yourself have the power to make yourself whole. That's not to say that you might not need some help along the way. That's why we have therapists, rehabilitation facilities, and yes, AA. Chronic alcohol abuse causes a plethora of physical and neurological damage, much of which can be healed over time. There are many fantastic resources to both learn more about and to address these concerns. A quick search on the internet can guide you to the appropriate resources.

You can find hope and create purpose in your life by learning and evolving in order reach your potential. You don't have to turn your life and will over to some outside source in order to do it. I take a somewhat existentialist view towards recovery and well-being in that you have to create the meaning in your life. For those who became addicted before they "grew up", there may never have been all that much meaning to begin with.

You have free will and the ability to think and decide how to use that gift. The fact that we have this freedom to choose rather than have our path dictated by instinct alone, is what separates us from all the other earthly creatures.

Your history is a factor

Unfortunately, even though we are self-determining entities, our past and the world that we are born into and currently inhabit, greatly influence the scope of options afforded to us.

In order to understand how we have arrived to our current state, it is imperative that we examine where we've been. While I am not advocating dwelling on the past and constantly reliving painful memories, our personal history, like it or not, has shaped and determined who we are today. We need to understand and embrace this part of our existence in order to re-claim our present and future lives. Unresolved issues from the past often cause you to become stuck and as a result, moving forward becomes extremely difficult at best. We obviously cannot change our history but we can certainly alter how we look at it and how we let it affect us.

Nobody asks to be born! Furthermore, you had absolutely no control over the circumstances of your beginnings. That part of your reality is chosen for you. Whether you were born rich/poor, black/white, religious/secular, your physical appearance, etc. are beyond any semblance of choice. These cultural, family, genetic, and economic histories very much influence the scope of choices that become available to you. That being said, even those who have been dealt a seemingly bad hand have the ability to overcome their current position. The world is filled with rags to riches stories of people who managed to overcome their disadvantaged beginnings and refused to be defined and held back by them. These success stories are by no means limited to material wealth or the attainment of a particular social standing. You have the ability to evolve and become rich in spirit and soul.

A very prevailing attitude towards life shared by many who are engulfed in the misery of addiction is that they have little control over their plight. They feel like pawns in the game of life and that the direction of their future has been mapped out for them. This feeling of despair has to be overcome!

Choose to choose/Decide to decide

Again, whether the feeling existed before you ever picked up your first drink or now that you've reached the end of your rope, a feeling of anxiety or unease seems to permeate the mind of almost every addict. It has become a nearly constant companion. Anxiety is simply an unease, or at its extreme, a genuine fear of the future. The extent of this unease can range from worrying about what the next moment will bring, to a fear of your future in general.

What causes this anxiety? For the majority of alcoholics it is an inability or refusal to make important decisions. Unfortunately, unless you live in a plastic bubble, making choices is an inevitable and constant aspect of life! These decisions that we make are often irreversible so making them can be painful and stressful. That these choices are irrevocable means that you can't take them back. That's scary stuff!

The problem is that try as you may, you can't completely avoid it. Even if you decide to follow a path of apathy and try to avoid making any meaningful choices, it's not possible because that in itself is a choice. You simply can't get away from this reality. In trying to do so, you are avoiding life!

Deciding to "choose" sobriety is HARD & SCARY!

Doing nothing is a very shallow and immature choice but one that alcoholics wholeheartedly embrace. There's a certain comfort level in being addicted. You don't have to decide to do anything besides chasing the next high, thereby reducing this horrible anxiety! You're like those dead zombies in those horror movies, only instead of mindlessly ambling towards the next fix of human flesh, you're just taking up time and space on your way to the next bottle.

Now that you understand a little bit about the anxiety and fear that come from the unknown results and ramifications of making choices, it should be easier to grasp the extent to which a great deal of courage is necessary to choose sobriety. You are entering a completely new and unknown world. This is your life and you deserve to have a good and fulfilling one. That's why I can't stress enough that you have to truly want it for you and not to appease anybody else. The world at large really doesn't care what you do, but you should! As the lead character, Andy Defresne, suggests in the brilliant movie, The Shawshank Redemption; you can either actively pursue living or you can give up, lose hope and fade away. Andy was an innocent man who broke out of jail and chose life; you can too! You can choose the freedom to recover!

Boredom and Idleness = Despair

Another common reason for drinking cited by many an alcoholic is a simple case of boredom. For the teenagers that never "decide" to partake in any extra-curricular activities like sports, band, clubs, etc., there is just way too much free time to kill. For some reason they don't develop any passion or drive to do anything more than what they have to. Usually there is a certain amount of guilt and emptiness in choosing to do nothing. Becoming a rebel without a cause by using drugs and alcohol creates what at the time seems like some kind of direction and goal. Granted the goal of attaining the next high isn't exactly a noble endeavor and it will lead to the further avoidance of decision making and living life in any kind of a meaningful way.

As adults, this boredom phenomenon often sets in as some people become disillusioned and frustrated by their roles in life. You have housewives and mothers who feel that their freedom to choose anything meaningful has been stripped away from them and thus they unconsciously turn to addiction where they become content in not having to make decisions. Yes, she still has to play her role, but she kind of goes about it on auto-pilot. The same type of transformation can take place for the career business person who loses passion for their job and begins to find it meaningless. So boredom sets in when you have either stopped shaping your own future out of choice or because you feel like that ability has been taken away from you due to the burdens of your daily existence and responsibilities. While these roles of parent and breadwinner are extremely important, they should not completely define and limit who you are as a person.

Deciding not to decide or choosing not to choose is both frustrating and BORING! It's like the kids sitting around after school who keep asking each other; "What do you want to do? The standard answer often being; "I don't know." This leads to idleness and boredom which can be very dangerous.

It's time to choose life!

Between this avoidance of life, any unresolved past issues and a feeling that you have no control over your own destiny, you can easily crash into despair, which is really just a lack of hope. In avoiding life, you've taken the stance that it's all just too scary and stressful and therefore not worth the risk. Your take on unresolved past issues is that they have left you as damaged goods and that's just the way it is. Finally, resigning yourself to the idea that the way you are and the way in which your life is presently constructed is written in stone, is a very fatalistic view. You are not a passive plant that has no control over its environment. Yes there are certain elements of your existence that are unchangeable but certainly not all of them. You alone have the power to overcome set obstacles, change how you view them and to determine your path going forward!

So you see, the past and your current indecisive state are places to learn and evolve from. Don't set up camp there because if you decide to live there, you're going to stay stuck! So let's move on. It's a new day full of hope and possibilities and you my friend are in the driver's seat. It's time to choose life.

Just a quick note here that while the first half of this book is primarily concerned with the pros and cons of AA, there is also a lot of good generic information regarding recovery. So it is worth reading even if you've already decided that their program is not for you. For example, when you decide to kick alcohol out of your life, you will be throwing your best friend to the curb. You will inevitably go through the grieving process which is discussed in Chapter two.

Justifiable Homicide

PS: Your friend? With friends like that who needs enemies! This so called friend, alcohol, is a selfish bastard that cares only about owning you. He's clearly succeeding because you've tossed away all of your other relationships to maintain your monogamous love-fest with him. If you really analyze what you are getting out of this relationship you will come to the conclusion that if there ever were any benefits to it, they're gone now. You would think that the damage that it causes to your overall health, your relationships and the tens of thousands of dollars that you have wasted on it would be enough to motivate you, but clearly it hasn't. Incarceration, the loony bin or death is where you are headed unless you file for divorce right now and walk out the door. So go ahead and grieve for this non-friend and then proceed to turn the tables and kick the bastard out of your life before he kills you!!!

What do you have to lose?

Actually the question here should be what do you have to gain? What you have to lose should be fairly clear at this point. If you haven't already lost jobs, spouses, friends and the respect of your children if you have any, just wait, because your present path will surely take care of that. Face it, it just isn't fun anymore. By choosing to end this sick affair you aren't depriving yourself of anything other than a downward spiral. Hopefully I've made my point and you don't have an intelligent comeback. So turn the page, both figuratively and literally.

Chapter 14

We're here, now what?

Ok, you've forgiven yourself for a condition that you had very little if any control over. So give yourself a clean slate and start anew. Why? Because you can and must if you are to become the self-determining person that you have always been meant to be.

If you are still feeling guilty about your past and the people you have hurt along the way, now is the time to put that behind you. The best way that you can make amends is by staying sober and proving it. No, it won't happen overnight. People's initial reaction will be one of ambivalence. Sure, they'll utter congratulatory phrases like, "That's great Laurie, good luck to you. I know you can do it." In reality they're thinking, "Yeah right, you're a lying alcoholic loser and you'll be drunk again in no time." Others will probably be a bit more compassionate and truly hope for your recovery. In either case, it could take months, even years before they believe that you have truly kicked your addiction. Still others may never again completely trust you no matter how long you've been sober. Looking at your track record, you can't really blame them. Is that fair? It doesn't matter, that's just the way it is. All you can do is the next right thing. If you can look at yourself in the mirror each night before you go to bed and be able to honestly tell yourself that you put your best foot forward, then that's good enough. People are going to judge you regardless. Stop caring so much about what "they" think of you. Stop trying to please others and be true to yourself. You don't need their affirmation as to what you are going to do with your life. If you think or worry about how others see you, that means that you believe you are lacking in some way. What way? Change it or accept it and stop it.

Don't accept what others have to say or what you observe without questioning it. Stop thinking that others are right and you are wrong. Your reality is your reality and you have the freedom and the responsibility to create and state it. You have the right to believe in it!

This whole worrying about what others think of you thing seems to be very pervasive among many alcoholics. Low self-esteem seems to be a common thread. Why do you think that people don't like you? In most cases it isn't even true. I personally suffered from this delusion for the majority of my life until I evolved past it in sobriety. To this day it can still rear its ugly head if I let it. A perfect example of this was when I was working for a company that had to eventually let me go because of my drinking. I was absolutely convinced that I just didn't fit in and that everybody in the organization thought badly of me and talked behind my back. During my exit interview, my district manager was almost brought to tears by having to let me go. His words to me went along the lines of; "Rolf, this is one of the most painful management decisions that I've ever had to make. You are one of the top sales people in the entire Northeast and everybody in this organization absolutely loves you." I left the building and walked to my car with my little box of personal effects in a state of total bewilderment. Again my inferiority complex took over and I told myself that he was just saying all that to make me feel good and that none of it was true. Well it must have been true as evidenced by the dozen or so calls that I received in the following weeks from people at all levels within the organization expressing their sincere shock and sorrow to hear of my departure.

Now to take a look at the flip side, let's say that people seriously don't like you. You have to ask yourself why?

There were times in my life when I made this irrational

fear come to life by acting in ways that would almost guarantee that people wouldn't like me. I would isolate myself and not participate or take an interest in the social fabric of an organization or in people in general. Should it then be any great surprise that people could take me or leave me and that I didn't form any close bonds?

Me, Me, Me

Once you've reached the point where the most important relationship in your life is the one between you and your booze, you can't help but to alienate yourself from everybody and everything else in the world. While it may not be your intent, you come across as indifferent or even worse, as arrogant, cocky, narcissistic, condescending or downright mean! People get the feeling that you really don't care about them and they are right because in reality you are incapable of doing so. You may be doing it unconsciously but you are pushing people away because they are getting in the way. Most people do, however, have a vague intuitive sense that this is going on but haven't the foggiest clue as to why. Once you decide to put the bottle down the reality that you are pretty much alone smacks you hard in the face. So how can you begin to reconnect to the world?

Don't just hear, listen!

If you are like a lot of alcoholics, your listening skills may not have been one of your greatest assets even before your drinking took off. One thing that is almost certain though, is that they got progressively worse as your drinking continued. I have covered this already but it is worthy of a revisit. There is a HUGE difference between listening and hearing! When you simply hear people speak, what you are basically doing is not paying attention to what they have to say and are just waiting for them to stop so that you can start talking again. Hearing is completely passive because you don't care what the other person thinks because it's all about you and you believe that you have all the answers anyway. You believe yourself to be this fantastically entertaining, social and funny speaker when in reality most people can't wait to find an excuse to leave because all you talk or care about is you, you, you!!!! Listening is an active SKILL and it is hard work. More importantly, listening requires empathy. You have to actually care about the other person and his or her opinions and beliefs. Try to understand and feel what they are experiencing and trying to convey. By stepping into their shoes you are sharing a piece of yourself and by doing so, you are becoming less self-involved. When you are just hearing, what you are actually doing is talking to yourself and anticipating what you are going to say next. Obviously you can't be listening when you are totally absorbed with your end of the conversation, if you can even call it that. Don't underestimate how brutally important it is to make a tremendous effort at changing this aspect of your demeanor, if it is in fact true in your case. Effective listening takes a long time to develop and is one area in my life where I know there is still much room for improvement. It makes all the difference in the world. When you care and show an interest in the rest of the universe, it has a funny way of doing the same in return! Listening is truly one of the most selfless and caring human activities and is one of the most useful skills that an alcoholic who truly wants to change his or her life can improve upon.

So once you have developed some empathy and are actively engaged with the world, you have earned the right to feel good about yourself! I have finally reached a point where, unless it's due to bad behavior or a poor attitude on my part, I simply don't care if people don't like me. This ambivalent attitude should not be seen as negative but rather as one of self-preservation and as a sign of maturity and growth.

That's enough about past mistakes and unhealthy attitudes for now. It's a new game and you're the GM, coach and quarterback. That's right; you're in control of the whole thing.

Does this have to be so hard and serious?

So you have to distance yourself from the past and re-create your new reality. Now you might be thinking that this is going to be very hard and you would be right. If you want easy street with no responsibility, have another drink. I don't mean to sound so serious but this is serious stuff. Life **is** serious and challenging but so worth living if you continually push yourself to new heights.

Your inclination here might be; "Screw this, I'd rather live in the moment without a care in the world, chill out and just have some fun." Well, up until this moment that's what you've been doing. How's that working for you? Your anxiety ridden, decision avoiding, isolating and meaningless way of approaching life has been pretty pathetic!

Look, I'm not trying to imply that your every waking moment should be goal and growth oriented. Everybody needs time to recharge their batteries and enjoy the fruits of their labor. There is great deal of wisdom in the old saying that there's a time and place for everything. There's nothing wrong with engaging in carefree activities like watching TV, gossiping with friends, playing, daydreaming, etc. as long as they're done in moderation and don't constitute your entire way of being.

Yes, you have to live life in the moment and be present, but you need to do it with purpose. If you don't have any aspirations and are just about immediate self- gratification, then you're like a rudderless boat going nowhere. A great quote by the renowned author E.B. White comes to mind; "I arise in the morning torn between a desire to improve the world and a desire to enjoy the world. This makes it hard to plan the day." You have to learn how to balance the two!

I think that one line very nicely sums up the one of the

great paradoxes of life. Our instinctual nature pulls us towards the things that are comfortable, easy and self-gratifying. Should I stay in bed with my new girlfriend or should I get up and fix that annoying leaky sink? Should I stop and help that old lady who has a flat tire or should I keep going because I don't want to miss the party? Should I go to class or should I finish my conversation on Facebook. Granted those 3 examples aren't exactly world changers but you get the idea.

So in deciding to participate in life and make meaningful choices, you have to fight from taking the easy route and continuously analyze from the plethora of options available. Pick the ones that truly matter! This of course requires discipline, effort and a desire to do the right thing. Most importantly, it requires that you think things through. In the end it's worth it because you don't end up second guessing your actions and having regrets. Well you still might, but at least you can feel good about the fact that those actions were undertaken after careful and painstaking consideration and not just on the fly or based on the guidelines of somebody or something else. Also, it is important to note that you can always change your course based on new insight and knowledge that you acquire in the process. Evolving isn't a static activity and by definition is one that is constantly in a state of change.

The key here is that deciding to decide is the healthy choice. It also has to be followed up with action; otherwise it's just an exercise in thinking hypothetically and is worthless.

So now you have this wonderful blank canvas with which you can create your own personal landscape full of endless of possibilities. Before you take action and embark on this limitless journey, you need to learn how to think better.

Chapter 15

The art of thinking

Your thoughts and the actions that follow are the paint that we use in the ever changing mosaic of life.

If you truly embrace the notion that you are not powerless then you also have to accept the responsibility that comes with free will and self-determination. Blind adherence to a higher authority is no longer the easy option. In fact, if you truly follow the path of self enlightenment, it's not really an option at all.

To a certain extent, you are what you think! If you believe yourself to be a loser, then as sure as the sun will rise, you will turn yourself into one. The reverse obviously holds true and if you have confidence in yourself and think that you are an important, meaningful and compassionate member of society, then good things and the respect of those around you, are highly likely to follow.

So what's drinking got to do with thinking?

While there are whole books dedicated to the topic of thinking, I hope to make the point in the following few pages, that how and what we think greatly affects the decision making process. This in turn dictates the actions which we take to form our mode of living and that create the meaning in our lives. Drinking alcoholically clearly affects our ability to think well, but even more importantly, it reduces our motivation to think at all!

Thinking about thinking!

I can't even begin to tell you how many times in AA meetings that I've heard people speak of the gerbil or hamster
wheel that reside in their heads. Only instead of a little rodent
spinning in endless cycles, it is really just an endless loop of
incessant and predominantly negative thoughts that seem to
have a life of their own. At its most extreme, this vicious cy-
cle can become so debilitating that you begin to feel like you
are on the verge of losing your mind. It's like there is a little
guy in your head calling all the shots and you have virtually
no control over the content. Prevailing themes to these patterns include obsessive guilty thoughts of past experiences,
paranoia or feelings of persecution, anxiety or fear about the
future, and just an overall aura of dread and hopelessness. At
the beginning stages of alcoholism, drinking slows the wheel
down somewhat and distracts the mind from going to these
dark places. Instead, a sense of euphoria and excitement in
pursuing activities that supply immediate gratification take
their place. The problem here is that eventually the band stops
playing, the party ends and you are left alone with your
thoughts. In the later stages of alcoholism, this temporary
feeling of relief becomes more and more fleeting, if it even
occurs at all.

On other occasions this spinning rodent wheel is consumed by daydreaming about things that could be, if only life
were fair. While these thoughts are generally about positive
and pleasant things in essence, the problem here is that we
spin the potential positive with the negative idea that it is beyond our grasp and that we don't have the tools necessary to
bring about these "dreams". That fatalistic negative feeling of
being unworthy and useless tends to quickly turn these potentially inspiring moments into more despair.

Doctor it hurts when I do this!

Most of us have heard the funny little story about when the guy hurts his arm and goes to the doctor's office and says, "Hey Doc, it hurts when I do this" (as he lifts his arm over his head). To which the doctor simply replies, "Then don't do that." Sounds simple right? Well it should be but for some reason most of us have this propensity for causing ourselves pain. Even after the doctor tells us to stop lifting our arm because it hurts, we still seem to do it just to make sure! So can't we just turn off these negative thoughts by refusing to think them? Well yes and no.

The little guys in our head

So who is responsible for putting this negative spin on our thought process? Well in a way, there really is a little guy, or several actually, that compete and have conversations as to which thoughts get priority in guiding and determining the decisions that follow. We all talk to ourselves! It's just that most of us do it non-verbally.

I've been known at times to be not so non-verbal which is why I adopted a cat so that people wouldn't think I'm crazy. In all seriousness, we all partake in these internal conversations constantly. Granted, a lot of these discussions are over fairly basic issues and lead to obvious courses of action. The internal banter isn't real deep and therefore doesn't cause much in the way of stress or anxiety. For example, when the alarm clock goes off in the morning you have to make the quick decision to either get up or start hitting the snooze button. The internal conversation is pretty quick, doesn't require much thought and probably will go something like this; "All right, time to get up and start the morning ritual so I can get out of here on time or I'm tired, think I'll hit snooze a few times and then hustle to get to work on time if I feel like it."

Even in this easy example, there is a you talking to a you. Just who are these guys? I like to call the guy who sifts through all these "internal voices" as the mediator or **arbitrator**. In a sense, he's the one, who after all debates are finished, that evaluates the possible choices and embarks on a course of action. He's the judge and jury if you will, while the guys that are pleading their case or cause are the attorneys or lobbyists. Using my silly alarm clock example we can see some of the opposing forces that come into play. On the one side you have the you that is responsible and understands and accepts that you need to get up, go to work and bring home a paycheck to help take care of your family needs and societal obligations. This you embraces the idea that you are part of a larger society that requires cooperation, sacrifice and doing your part in order to make the whole thing work. On the opposite side of the equation lays the you that just really doesn't give a damn. This is the guy who wants to hit the snooze button and sleep in and gravitates towards laziness, immediate self-gratification and a feeling of entitlement. For the mature, responsible, and conscientious person, chances are that the arguments of the lobbyist who is advocating getting out of bed and getting motivated are going to win out. For the alcoholic, the lawyer who is all about entitlement and doing whatever you feel like is likely to have more pull with the arbitrator. So as you can see, from the moment we open our eyes in the morning, the wheel starts spinning.

Life's big questions

It's not the easy questions like should we have toast or cereal for breakfast that cause us the biggest stress. It's our internal reflections as to whether or not we made the right decision yesterday or the anxiety of making the right choices for today and tomorrow which cause us to question whether or not we are doing the right things in life. It's not generally a healthy idea to spend too much time either romanticizing or resenting the past or worrying about or constantly anticipating the future. When you engage in too much past or future thinking, you can actually think too much.

So is there a healthy way to stop this evil wheel of despair and doubt or to at least slow it down to manageable levels? Well as a matter of fact there is and it can be summed up nicely in one word.

Action

Taking action implies that you are doing something. If you are just "thinking" you're not doing. Again you are choosing not to choose which promotes inactivity. It requires guts and courage to be present and active. Beyond thinking, what really determines who you are, are the actions that result from the choices that you make based on your thinking. You need to have some goals in order to create purpose and meaning to your life.

All of these gerbil wheel non-activities that take place in your head keep you from being present in your life. The here and now is where life happens and is the only place where you can take the action necessary to affect the changes required to be a self-determining soul or entity.

The anxiety that is felt from taking action is normal and should not be seen as negative. It's just a natural state that arises when facing the inevitable fact that choices need to be made. As discussed previously, these decisions can be painful and difficult, with results and consequences that are not entirely in our control or predictable.

It's the unknown results and a fear of failure that cause the anxiety. Of course the more you think about the possibility of failing, the more likely it is to occur. It's a self-fulfilling prophecy. If you don't develop some sense of purpose for which you are willing to take some risks, then life can very easily lose its meaning which can then in turn lead to despair, loss of hope, etc... Instead of predicting failure, spin it and utilize the power of positive thinking! Success or failure is most often a direct result of one's attitude. Envision yourself as being empowered to succeed instead of feeling sorry for yourself and predicting negative results. Replace self-pity with confidence!

What kind of goals or purpose should we strive for?

Try to blend and vary your goals. Some should be strictly personal and be attainable and quantifiable to an extent. A personal goal can be something as simple as vowing to attend all of your kids' sporting events or having dinner together as a family. Just keep in mind that the kids will grow up and new goals and purpose always need to be cultivated. Other goals, however, could be way beyond your capability to accomplish as an individual alone and be those in which you work together towards a common goal. Such things as world peace or ending hunger in your county are lofty goals of which you can be an enduring and constant contributor. These kinds of goals help you to connect with the world around you, get you out of your isolation and create meaning in your world. Whatever you choose, be passionate about it and believe that it is important, attainable and that it truly matters! We all need to have a sense of purpose otherwise that hamster wheel just keeps on turning!

Could've, should've, would've

One of the biggest ways by which you keep the wheel spinning is by obsessing over hypotheticals. Going over and over what one could have done in a past situation or contemplating how things might have turned out differently if this or that happened, doesn't change the reality of the present situation. Sure you should analyze what happened and then take any appropriate action that might make things better in the present and/or future. Do that and move on! Stop continuously revisiting what is already done. By not moving forward you get stuck on the carrousel of incessant and non-productive thought.

Own the job of arbitrator and put the lawyers on retainer!

The problem with the little guys in our head is that even though we can be aware of their existence and of the fact that they are trying to influence our decision making, we can't entirely shut them up. The good, the bad and the ugly are all part of everybody's make up and we can't wish them away. What you can do as an educated and moral arbitrator is to weigh the merits of their arguments and then make a binding decision and follow through on it. As the arbitrator you have the final say on who you will let occupy space in your head.

So when you hear the negative thought purveyors come knocking on your door, realize that they have been sent by that annoying prosecutor who wants to punish you for crimes you did not commit. Even if you did something not so nice, the prosecutor wants to dole out punishment that far exceeds the seriousness of the transgression. Basically, he wants you to beat the crap out of yourself. Recognize it immediately and say to yourself, "Oh, it's you again! Sorry the lights are on but nobody is home for you, I'm not buying into your negativity!

Painful thoughts that pre-occupy you

Pre-occupation often has one major element; Non-acceptance of how it is. Inevitably it will be about something you wish you could change but can't. By not accepting some fact, you can't let it go and therefore think of little else, which is not good. It usually has a time element involved as well. You can't help but think how this situation or person has caused you pain in the past or how this situation or person is affecting your present feelings. You are afraid of how it will be resolved going forward.

Yes, the noisy attorneys will get their chance to state their case at which point you need to either validate or dismiss their opinions and incorporate the salient point in your decision. These guys are paid well and they will be back; but you can develop the power to make them take a mandatory break once in a while! These naysayers are extremely patient and persistent but there are things that you can do to give the arbitrator in you more power.

Give the arbitrator (you) a rest!

Take a break! Thinking is exhausting and hard work. Incessant thinking is absolutely taxing and can mentally and emotionally wipe you out. Just like your body needs rest and time to re-charge itself, the mind is no different. Thinking too much, whether it's about everyday stuff or the big questions of meaning, can leave you emotionally drained. One method of quieting the mind is to take the time to practice some form of **meditation**. Meditation is a tricky subject because it has so many meanings that can range from "thinking deeply" to "not consciously thinking at all". It can also be religious or secular in nature. Regardless of which way you lean or which definition you embrace, a common thread of all meditation is that the practice of it is an attempt to distance yourself in some way from the automatic, ritualized and incessant thinking that we've been discussing.

Another way in which people have found themselves getting off of the rodent wheel of thought is by entering **"the zone"**. The zone is a place where people find themselves lost in non-thought when exerting themselves physically. Long distance runners routinely report of arriving there and experiencing a "runners high." Whole blocks of time can pass without conscious thought when in this state. I have personally experienced glimpses of this phenomenon when snow skiing and even longer durations while kayaking. It is extremely liberating and relaxing all at the same time.

Perhaps the most enjoyable method I can think of for giving your mind a break is to engage in some good old fashioned **sex**! Besides the extreme physical pleasure of experiencing an orgasm, the other thing that makes sex so great and spiritual is that it takes you off of the rodent wheel of thought. If you're thinking about your promotion or the argument you had with your kid then it can't be that good and you might consider a new partner! (That was a joke folks) Just keep in mind that like all other "fun" activities, the pursuit of sexual gratification should be done in moderation. You can become addicted to sex which is the last thing that you need.

Alcoholic drinking is NOT the way to give your mind a rest!

I mentioned it at the beginning of the chapter but it bears repeating. Alcoholic drinking kills the desire to think and make decisions and diminishes your ability to do so. Drinking puts you in a zone alright, just not "the zone" but more like the ozone!!!!! I said your mind needs the occasional rest, not a permanent vacation!!!!!

Other tools to help the arbitrator (you)

As the boss in this internal struggle, arm the good guys with the tools necessary to become the dominant voices. Let's call the internal good guys your defense attorneys because they are in direct opposition to the prosecutors who continuously try to make you feel guilty, or trick you into committing stupid offenses or doing things against your nature. One thing you can do for the preferred team is to arm them with a set of **goals** or a **plan** if you will. If you know what you want to accomplish and where you want to go, then the chances and likelihood of negative thinking creeping in is greatly reduced. Writing these aspirations down is an extremely powerful way in which to give them priority status in the avalanche of thoughts competing to be heard. **"To do lists"** are extremely practical and help keep you focused on positive endeavors. This is particularly important during the early stages of sobriety when you are very likely to be at a loss as to what to do with all of your new found time.

Healthy Body/Healthy Mind

Besides the possibility of entering the "zone", **exercising** improves your stamina and energy levels thus making you feel much more vibrant. It's so much easier for the negative forces to grab a hold of you when you are feeling exhausted and empty. The flip side of that naturally is that when you feel good and energetic your chances of being upbeat and motivated go way up.

By the time you make the decision to turn your life around and get sober, the chances are that you have let your body get run down and out of shape. The extent to which you can embark on an exercise program is dependent upon many factors and you should consult with your doctor before doing anything too ambitious.

The role of Nutrition

It is indeed the very rare alcoholic who eats well. I personally rarely ate breakfast and lunch was often the only time I really ate for the entire day. The unique problem that alcohol poses is that in a sense, it is food! It is full of calories and when you are drinking you simply aren't hungry! Needless to say that if your main source of caloric intake is provided by booze then your ability to think rationally is going to be compromised to say the least.

Prolonged alcohol use alters one's brain chemistry and causes all sorts of physical problems. For some reason, the recovery "professionals" and the public in general, would rather pretend that none of that stuff is a factor and would rather just keep pounding away at the idea that those who suffer from alcoholism are simply weak willed and can be saved by AA.

At the end of the day, recovery **is** largely a question of will, but there are so many factors that affect our ability to use our will to its full potential. Thankfully, there are methods we can utilize to improve those abilities and overcome those obstacles.

So, in conclusion as to my thoughts on thinking, while you don't have total control of the thoughts that will come into your head, you do have many ways in which to influence those that will be dominant and move you to action. Using the tools and ideas that I have outlined will help you navigate and control the wide stream of thoughts that are constantly jumping onto the wheel. Remember that ultimately you are the boss and can develop the power to greatly dictate what goes on up there. It's not about how much or how little you think; it's about what you choose to think about and what you do with it. It's time to use that wonderful gift of free will and start creating the life that you choose with enthusiasm and wonderment.

Chapter 16

Life happens now!

OK, so let's assume that you are now thinking well and are ready to start living the life that you deserve. When should you start doing this? How about right now? Life happens now, right here, right now!

Not to beat a dead horse here but I think it is vitally important to once again point out that to live your life in the present with purpose is the polar opposite of Bill Wilson's fundamental AA principle of living life "one day at a time". That way of existing emphasizes dwelling on your guilty and sinful past along with fearing your future if you don't embrace and immerse yourself in the AA culture and live by its steps (suggestions). Holding on for dear life is what most recovering alcoholics in AA must do. **You** don't drink anymore so therefore **you** are not a recovering anything! If you want to go to an AA meeting to see some friends and hang out with some non-drinking folks that's fine, but don't do it because you "have to" in order to stay normal. Rip off the AA bandage and start living without guilt, regrets and in a constant state of fear or unease.

As previously stated, the best way to keep from overthinking all the time is to become actively engaged in doing. Sure the mind is still thinking whenever you are completing tasks but the emphasis is more on being efficient in what you are doing as opposed to contemplating the whys and meaning of it all. Just thinking about it doesn't cut it. Doing happens not in the past or in the future but in the present. At the end of the day, that's where we live our lives or should in any case!

Life is just a series of nows. The now now, the nows then and the nows that haven't happened yet. They all play an important role in the big picture but the one that is happening now is the only one that is real. It is also the one in which you have the most control over.

Living in the present with purpose means that you won't have to question yourself all the time. Yes, at first it might mean just getting through the day without having a drink. The one day at a time thing is OK at the beginning of recovery; just don't make it a lifetime habit because life has soooo much more to offer. Obviously living life one day at a time the AA way is better than living it drunk. In the long run, however, it still is pretty unfulfilling and sad if you need to do so just in order to "survive" the day.

Don't regret the past or fear the future. The past has led you to be who you are today. Learn from and use it but then let it go. Resentments keep you locked in the past. You can't be present if you are consumed by your resentments. You need to heal the past so that you can move forward and evolve. Negative events from your past only have as much power to influence your present to the extent that you let them. If you hold on to them they will keep you stuck. If they are still in play and are affecting present circumstances then you need to confront the issues and change them if you can. If you can't then you must either forgive and accept the transgressors or cast them away. In either case, you have to assign some form of closure to the past or you will have no peace from it.

The idea that everything happens for a reason is very romantic and it is easy to use that as an excuse for your current state of affairs. A more useful approach is to realize that things in life simply happen and that it is up to you to create what the meaning of those events will be in your present life and how they will affect your plans going forward.

Bad things happen to good people

Even more damaging than trying to live in yesterday's victories or glory is letting painful memories or unfulfilled promises negatively influence your current and future state of mind. The only way you're going to negate the effects of a negative history is to use the wisdom learned or gained by such experiences. Turn that knowledge into a positive influence that guides you in making better decisions going forward. This is of course easier said than done but is necessary to have any kind of contentment in your life. Sometimes yesterday's hurts are buried so deep that one may need professional help to bring them to the surface. This is often true in cases where one has suffered mental or physical abuse. In many instances, people who suffered this kind of trauma often somehow blame themselves for the injustices bestowed upon them. Forgive yourself and see yourself as the innocent person that you are.

There are those who also believe that in order to truly move on that one must forgive those who have caused them pain. This is obviously extremely difficult and goes against our survival nature but it truly is the best way to give the hurtful experience closure. One way to do this is to look at the transgressor as damaged goods. I believe most people are born good but that various influences ranging from family, economic opportunities, dysfunctional living situations in their own lives, etc. contribute to turning one into an evil being. Think of them as not having been able to stop themselves from hurting you. In this way you can forgive both parties and close this dark chapter in your life. I'm not implying that you won't dislike this person or hate what they did to you, but if you look at the hurt as having been caused by someone that is deranged, then it becomes a little easier to bear. If you can't forgive the person, then for your own good, at least forgive their actions and their effect on you. Bad things happen to good people!

Having suffered from horrid abuse or from a single tragic event I believe further strengthens the argument that things just happen and not necessarily for any specific reason. I mean what kind of God or benevolent universe would thrust such circumstances upon its people? Maybe the purpose of such happenings is to teach us to take any negative chain of events and see them as a lesson showing that life is hard and not always a warm and fuzzy place. You need to develop the fortitude to be strong enough to deal with anything that is thrown at you.

You Can't Stop and Smell the Roses All the Time

Why do today what I can put off until tomorrow is a very lazy, unfulfilling and ultimately depressing way to live. Alcoholics tend to live their lives this way with a "dude, what's the hurry, where's the fire" type of attitude. They have no sense of urgency about anything and therefore absolutely nothing gets done! Living in the present does not mean to stop and smell the roses all the time. Yes, you do need to regularly stop and appreciate the wonderful aspects of life and the beauty that surrounds you, but not to the point of complacency. One AA slogan with which I totally agree is that one should develop an "attitude of gratitude".

The world is a fantastic place and you should take the time to appreciate all that is good. Hopefully you have some great memories but keep them in perspective and understand that you can't live on the past's happiness! It just doesn't work that way. The more you try to wish it to be that way the more miserable you make yourself. Taking time to reflect and even meditate is necessary to maintain a sense of calm and to make sure you don't get caught up in that gerbil wheel of thought. It is important, however, to take stock of where you are and to evaluate whether or not you are on track towards accomplishing the goals that you have set. Again, if you haven't set any aspirations going forward you need to do so;

otherwise it is almost impossible to live with purpose in the present. It becomes way too easy to slip into mourning for a past that is gone.

Reflecting and meditating is great but stuff still has to get done. Being a Buddhist monk who can sit around all day and meditate might sound nice and relaxing but for the most part, the majority of people can't and don't want to live that way. Not to mention, it doesn't pay the bills. Life is full of responsibilities and work! That's just the way it is. For some reason alcoholics seem to think that all of the demands that life presents are somehow unfair. It's as if they believe that they should be entitled to an easy life. It's that mindset or sense of entitlement that has kept many an alcoholic from sufficiently growing up and being responsible for the course of their lives. The old "poor me" attitude sets in and life just becomes one ongoing attempt to avoid pain and to seek relief through drugs and alcohol which, as we know, doesn't work in the long run.

Life presents us with never ending challenges which in turn create stress. When confronted with stressful situations (life), alcoholics very quickly turn to the bottle to avoid dealing with it. The non-alcoholic mature individual has developed life skills such as adaptation and acceptance with which to handle stress.

When you know what you stand for and live your life with conviction in the present, then fear and anxiety tend to lose their grip on you.

This is a bit of a paradox but whereas life is very serious, you shouldn't take it so seriously. By that I mean that in the present, you should act with deliberate intent in an organized and serious manner. However, you should not take the **results** of these actions so seriously. You do your best at any given moment and if the end results aren't quite what you were looking for then don't berate yourself over it. Instead make adjustments now that will yield better results later. More importantly, whatever you do, don't worry about what those results are going to be! Worry=Stress! Stress about the future is one of the biggest triggers to addictive behavior that exists.

Just a side note here; I'm not suggesting that you never do anything spontaneously. That might sound like it contradicts doing things in a purposeful and methodical manner but it really doesn't. Being spontaneous, just like stopping to "smell the roses", is extremely beneficial and results in inner peace and joy. The point is that even when you decide to do something on the fly, do it with passion! Get totally immersed in it and don't worry about where it's leading.

But I'm too stressed out to live in the moment!

Really? When do you feel stress? In the moment that you are in! Stress almost always rears its ugly head in response to events past, present and future. Things that keep us from living in the moment include dwelling about resentments and anger over people, places and events (the past) or stressing about things that have yet to occur (the future). I've covered a lot of ground on what to do with the past and will attempt to put the final nail in that coffin in the next chapter dealing with acceptance and change.

Why do we stress over the future? The biggest reason is because it deals with unknown results which in turn cause fear and anxiety. Think about it, have you ever been nervous about a job interview or a first date? You are worrying about what "might" happen. Of course some of those possibilities include getting hurt, losing, etc... Even if you are confident that the results will be good, you can't be sure. Good or bad, you are obsessing about a future that does not yet exist and by doing so you are causing yourself stress by not being grounded in the present.

The other reason why we avoid residing in the present is due to the feeling that we are not good enough right now and that our only hope is in a future that is "better". That's a lot of pressure to throw at a future that doesn't yet exist! As a result of this feeling of unease and uncertainty, many addicts try to fill this void with drugs and alcohol. Non-addicts do the same thing with money, power, fame, possessions, etc... The problem is that the pleasure derived from attaining the powerful job title, the expensive yacht or the next great high is very fleeting and that feeling of lacking or non-wholeness comes right back into place. The term "chasing the dragon" refers to this elusive pursuit of a "high" that will bring you that feeling of contentedness or wholeness. Again the problem is that once it's here, it's gone as fast as it came and you have to go on chasing it all over again. That's why alcoholics and addicts are obsessed with the near future. You know, like one minute, five minutes or an hour from now. You are always anticipating what that next shot or drink will bring. You think, "Ahh, when I get that next bottle all will be good in the world". Again, you simply are not content in the present; you're counting on that next (near future) drink to bring you peace. Of course that peace never comes because when you finally get the bottle and take a shot, the feeling of fulfillment or contentedness is already fading not long after it reaches the pit of your stomach! Before you know it you're already planning, whether consciously or not, your next drink. When it finally comes, the whole chain starts all over again with no happiness in the moment and the promise of contentment in the near future being just an ugly and cruel lie! In a very real sense, those who are addicted can't find peace in the moment.

You need to cultivate an appreciation for the moment without any profound expectations. Allow it and yourself to just BE. Are you in a state of panic or dread as you are reading this? Probably not, because you are in the moment, absorbing these ideas and not forecasting some future event or reliving some past debacle.

Detachment is the present's most powerful tool

So just how do we manage to stay present and live in the moment? One of the most effective tools for doing so is to cultivate the ability to detach yourself from what is happening. Detachment involves experiencing the moment by kind of observing what's happening without a sense of personal ownership or responsibility. The emphasis is more on letting the events unfold as opposed to dictating how that will take place. It's going with the flow or rather, letting the flow happen. You still have a large part in it but it's not ALL about you. You still have to go about living with a sense of purpose and intention but don't get all caught up in the possible results. In other words, don't get overly involved with how you got there (past) or what the outcome will be (future). Just do your part and let the rest happen on its own momentum. Life in many ways is a game and the old saying; "It doesn't matter if you win or lose, it's how you play the game" is spot on. If you are "thinking" about winning or losing, then you aren't totally present in the game.

As far as present moment stress goes, it is also often the result of things not having gone your way (recent past). Again, nobody ever said that they were going to or that they were supposed to! The world just works that way sometimes. The world isn't necessarily cruel and out to get you, it just is. At the end of the day, for the most part, the world just doesn't care about every little decision we have to make. As human beings, we are the only species that is smart enough or maybe as the case may be, dumb enough, to think that it should! If you become more proficient in practicing detachment, then stress won't have anywhere to enter the equation. If you are totally present then there is no room for the past and future and the stress that comes along with it.

Stress is all about time!

Whether it was something that happened years ago, moments ago, something that is about to happen or that will down the road, it all revolves around time. Remove time's power and influence from your life and you will find it much less stressful.

Besides learning to live in the moment, other mature ways of handling the stresses of life are the subject of the next chapter which revisits acceptance and change.

Chapter 17

Acceptance and change

OK, all this talk about living in the present is probably annoying if the present is miserable. If the present isn't cutting it, obviously you need to do something about it. If you haven't got the point yet, it's all that we ever really have. Acceptance has been mentioned throughout the book but now it is time to really bring home its importance, in terms of both your addiction and your life in general.

You can't drink...Period...

Read the above line 5000 times if that's what it takes. Read it, believe it and accept it!

After a period of abstinence from alcohol your mind will try to convince you that you are over the hump and that you are now OK to join happy hour. Why does it try and do this? Because getting high feels good!!!!!

Too bad!

Your brain chemistry has been tweaked! I don't care if you have been sober for 12 years; you have a switch somewhere in your head that can't be turned off. Your logic tries to convince you that since you've been "good" for xyz amount of days, months, or whatever, that you now have the resolve to call it quits when you should. That's what I thought when I rationalized that celebrating not having a drink for a year was worthy of a few good shots of vodka! After all, I earned it right? That's how crazy the addictive mind can be.

This time around, even though I believe that I have matured, learned how to live better, etc., I haven't tested the waters because I know exactly what the inevitable results will be. I ACCEPT the fact that my brain and body will not permit me to be a reasonable and responsible social drinker.

Does that suck? Not anymore. Because I've accepted the reality of MY condition and I have been able to change how I deal with life and be happy with it! At the end of the day that is the key to recovery. If being high or drunk remains more desirable than the alternative of being sober, then there will be no incentive to change your way of life. You need to transform your ideologies so that alcohol free living becomes as much, if not more fun and satisfying than getting wasted.

So what's so great about being high?

Ok, so we all know that getting drunk makes you feel good. The question is why? Because being under the influence blocks out all the un-pleasantries of life. Chores like work, parenting, paying the bills, etc.; if you bother with them at all, become less daunting and stressful. Actually, it's not so much that they become less demanding, rather that you just alter your mental state so that you simply don't deal with these responsibilities in a mature and rational manner. The biggest lure, however, is the anesthetizing effects that mind altering drugs have on any emotional and mental anguish from which you may be suffering. With all that "stuff" covered up, what's left is a feeling of euphoria, freedom, and bliss. What's not to like? The problem is that it's not sustainable. That "stuff" that you are blocking out is still there and when you come down it is all still waiting for you. Add to that the fact that the body can't and won't take it indefinitely and you may be able to appreciate that there needs to be another way. And just what is that other way?

Don't drink, don't worry and be happy!

Ok, so how do we get there?

We've covered some important ideas already such as reducing stress and worry by not obsessing about the future, living in the moment, letting go and forgiving yourself and your past, developing better listening and thinking skills, and embracing decision making thereby determining your own path. We're almost ready to explore the ways of living that will not only make it tolerable but that will transform it into the glorious dance that it is meant to be. But first, a reality check.

It is what it is

Right now we'll discuss an idea that has also been embraced by AA and which is essential for moving forward, namely, accepting life on life's terms. This encompasses the past, present and future and how we relate to them all because that's what constitutes our existence.

Everybody has underlying pain, guilt and issues. We've all committed "sins" as none of us are perfect. It's a matter of our maturity and willingness to accept and initially live with the guilt; but then to eventually evolve, forgive ourselves and then move on. Accept the things that we cannot change, change the things that we should if we can and free ourselves of the pain, guilt and bondage. Is it going to go away? No, it's reality. Pain and suffering are a part of the human condition. Anyone who thinks and expects that we deserve not to have any, is delusional. It's not the way it is. It's the mechanism by how we grow if we let it. Accept it and deal with it. If you feel guilty about something and you can make some of that guilt go away by making amends and doing the next right thing, then by all means, that's what the mature soul wants us to do. The immature ego that is in denial is going to rear its ugly head and try to bury it in its subconscious because it can't face it. As a result, you as keeper of that wounded soul, are likely to help keep it there through denial or even worse, artificially via drugs and alcohol.

Show some humility and admit fault

Denial is simply a defense tactic. Your belief system is being attacked and your instinct is to protect it. It's the old, "not me, I didn't do it". You want to believe that it isn't a problem but it is. So you try and rationalize it away. It's denial of the truth and an escape from responsibility. Admit it, face up to it, and you can turn the tide.

Healing residual pain

Now that we've addressed accepting those things in which we played a direct role, what are we to do with those horrible pains and tragedies that follow us through no fault of our own? Earlier I mentioned that bad things happen to good people. What's up with that? Why? The only answer that makes any sense to me is that it is a direct result from the forces of evil. Evil is unfortunately a necessary component of our universe. For without it, there can be no good; we need the contrast in order to see, experience and appreciate it. So what do we do with it when it invades our space? The only thing that we can do is use it as the life learning tool that it is meant to be. If you let it tear you down, then despair, depression and very possibly addiction can hardly be unexpected. We kill evil by not letting it win. We evolve into the loving, forgiving, altruistic beings that evil cannot stand. Doing so won't make all the hurt go away but it will take away its power over us.

Can we beat down all of the evils of the world? Well, individually it is asking too much. Collectively, everybody doing their part, the sky is the limit. So what, you may ask, is your part? Simply to do the next right thing and embrace the fact that you are an important member of the world and that we are all in this together. Addiction is a selfish condition where no happiness can be found! By giving of yourself freely, you can alter your course and be the positive life force that you were intended to be.

Change is not only unavoidable and good, but necessary!

As previously discussed, life is full of an endless series of choices and decisions. It is inevitable that many of these decisions will result in some kind of change. As such, this is a good time to revisit Mr. Niebuhr's Serenity Prayer which goes as follows; "God, give us the grace to accept with serenity the things that cannot be changed, courage to change the things that should be changed, and the wisdom to distinguish the one from the other."

So the ever important question then, is what things should we try and change? How are we to know? One way is obviously to utilize all of the tools listed earlier. One not so obvious resource for trying to determine the areas in which we should try to exert influence comes from deep within. I am of course talking about intuition; that place that does not necessarily conform to logic or careful thought. To let our intuition guide us is clearly an act of faith. As the saying goes, "always trust your intuition". It may not always seem like the prudent course but it is always authentic. More times than not, both your intuition and a logical approach, will be in harmony with one another. When it comes to addiction, common sense and your inner voice are both telling you that this way of being is extremely damaging and hurtful to both yourself and the world at large. You wouldn't be reading this if it wasn't true! Addiction causes a negative life force that is at odds with your true nature. So you have to negate its power.

It's time to re-join the Human Race

So we know that change is inevitable but what then is its true purpose? How do we use it as a constructive tool and not just change for change's sake. We do so by making decisions not because they are inevitable but because they will foster growth and understanding, thereby enabling you to exhibit love, compassion and empathy.

The most powerful tool that you have to combat the selfish nature of addiction is to extend yourself for the betterment of mankind and to conduct yourself in a selfless manner! Freedom equals the love and nurturing of your fellow man.

Chapter 18

Selflessness

Addiction is a soul sapping affliction that takes you away from your very own human nature. It renders your ability to give and receive love null and void. In many ways, you receive in life what you are willing to extend of yourself. Addiction is a take, take, take, me, me, me form of living death because it strips you of your ability to empathize, feel, love, to care. It is said that no man is an island and I believe that to be true. Human beings are social animals that cannot thrive by themselves. There is nothing wrong with being what would be termed a private person. That is a far cry from being a hermit who has closed off as much communication with the outside world as possible. Being private and having only a small network of friends, family or people in your life is fine; as long as you are willing to give of yourself to the world and those in your circle. It is essential that you allow yourself the vulnerability of possibly getting hurt along the way. That is simply because when you give of yourself to another, there is the possibility that what you give will not be reciprocated or that it will not be appreciated by the one on the receiving end. Do it anyway! By doing so, chances are that you will be in alignment with your soul. To give of yourself without an expectation of return is the truest form of selflessness there is and is one in which you will not be hurt in the process. If you truly do not expect anything in return for your acts of generosity or empathy, than there can be no response that will hurt you.

Why living by the Golden Rule
isn't always enough

On the face of it, living by the Golden Rule; "Do unto others as you would have them do unto you", would appear to take care of the whole selflessness issue. I believe it was the 19th century German philosopher, Friedrich Nietzsche, who posed the question; "What then happens when a masochist follows the Golden Rule?" You see the problem? If that were the case, to treat others as you would have them treat you would mean exhibiting cruelty and causing pain! So you have to rise above everything and accept the ideal of creating the greatest good for everybody. It means extending ourselves beyond the self interest of our ego. Not that you are likely to be a masochist but the point is that you have to go beyond treating people as a mirror of your own desires and wants. You have to treat them in ways that foster their growth and well-being regardless of whether or not it's what you want or how it affects you. While the benefits of doing so may not initially seem all that apparent, in the long run, you will feel better about yourself.

Stop being a no-show

Life is not a spectator sport! In order for it to have any meaning, you have to play. It is a point that cannot be understated. Life in many ways is a game played with others and you can't participate if you aren't there. And while showing up and watching is better than hiding at home or in your head, to truly find joy and embrace life, you have to actively take part. Does this again leave you vulnerable? Well yes it does because there is a good chance that you may "lose" any particular game. That's when it's important to remember that it is only a game and it will be followed by a "new" game where you start off again on equal footing. This again goes back to the idea that I suggested in which you give the present moment all of your concentration and determination but you then accept the results and don't take them so personally or seriously. You're a winner just by playing! You really can't lose when you think about it because if you come up short that means that somebody else was victorious. So your "sacrificing" a win gives somebody else the joy of tasting success. So that in and of itself, is a kind of victory.

You don't have to isolate and be alone

By the time you reach the point in your addiction that you are honestly ready to do something about it, chances are that you have alienated most people in your life and have even convinced yourself that you prefer your own company. This is largely a result of the fact that nobody wants to be around you much anyway. Towards the end, you yourself just want to be left alone with your bottle. Rejoining the world is hard. It takes courage, determination and patience.

Be kind to yourself, it takes time. You might slip and have a relapse or several. It's OK! This isn't AA; you don't have to start "counting" again. Life is now. So you just start over again now! That's it. Do not beat yourself up; you have not failed at anything! We are works in progress and always will be. You are taking responsibility for getting yourself well and you should be proud of that.

Finding meaning through altruism and empathy

Some people are lucky enough to find meaning through their vocation. Doctors, nurses, teachers, social workers, etc. all give of themselves and most do so because they find it rewarding. You may be saying to yourself, yeah, but they get paid. So what? We all have to make living in this world, that's how it works.

Others find it in their station in life. The stay at home

mom who dedicates her life to the welfare of her children and is fulfilled in doing so, doesn't question her value. If she desires more during the process and/or after they have sprouted their wings and left the nest, the opportunities to serve are endless.

What about those who work tirelessly in a job that they simply do not like but continue to do so because they embrace their responsibility to provide for themselves and those that they love? They too have options to create more meaning in their lives. It is never too late to learn new skills and re-invent yourself. Then there are the endless opportunities to give back outside of the framework of your vocation.

Volunteer your time

Just the fact that you are reading this book means that you possess a gift that can be a godsend to someone else. The ability to read is a gift taken for granted by most. Organizations like Literacy for America offer you the opportunity to share that amazing ability with those less fortunate than yourself.

The scope and variety of ways in which you can give of yourself are endless. Hospitals, nursing homes, animal and homeless shelters are forever in need of the selfless service given freely by their volunteers.

Instead of just watching your son or daughter participate in extra-curricular activities, offer to be mentor or coach.

Several months after I beat this affliction, I volunteered at my local fire department. Due to a condition of claustrophobia caused by a traumatic childhood experience I could not stay, but I put myself out there. Experiment with different options and you might find something that gives you that feeling of making a difference.

Hey, I'm not saying that volunteering is something that you have to do, but if you have the time and are so inclined, it is a kind and selfless endeavor that will definitely leave you feeling good about yourself.

Simple everyday kindness is huge

You may scoff at this thought but simple things like offering your seat on a bus to an elderly or physically challenged person is an act of kindness that can't be understated.

When you are at the checkout counter paying for your groceries, take notice of the person's name (they are usually wearing name tags) and say; "Thank you Jane, have a great day". Just try it. You will see their world get a little brighter if even only for a few seconds. It makes a difference and it's easy! More importantly, it's simply the right thing to do and the right way to be. You can't help but feel better about yourself by doing so. That shouldn't be your motivation but it is certainly the end result.

Listen and care

I know that I've touched on this already but it warrants another look within the context of selflessness. One of the greatest acts of kindness or caring that you can offer someone is that of truly listening to them. You may be thinking, what's the big deal, that's easy. Nothing could be farther from the truth. Most people, alcoholics and addicts in particular, are completely obsessed with what is going on in their little corner of the world. They pretend to be listening with interest but in reality they barely even hear most of what is said. Sure you can fake it but you really aren't kidding anybody and most importantly, you know that you don't care. It's ironic because so many alcoholics complain that they are misunderstood and that nobody really likes them. Well, if you don't give a damn about other people, why in Hell should they care about you? I don't mean to sound cruel here but that's the bottom line. Do you want to have an interesting and social life? If so, the only way you can authentically do that is to actually take an interest in the lives of other people. Try and see things from their point of view and attempt to have "real" conversations. If you do this, you will see your isolation begin to disappear right before your very eyes. It is far from easy. Good listening is a SKILL and you have to want to develop it in order to engage in sincere and meaningful discourse.

Besides being self-absorbed, alcoholics/addicts often tend to think that they know it all and are always right. That's one of the major reasons why they don't or even can't empathize with others. If you honestly think that your take on things is the only right one, then it is easy to see why you don't care about the opinions of those around you. Even if you are smarter than everybody else, which is probably far from the truth, you need to both value and consider other people's viewpoints.

On the flip side, another reason why you may choose to isolate and avoid intimate conversations and connections with others may actually be the exact opposite of thinking that you know it all. While some alcoholics have this unhealthy need to be right all the time and actually believe that they are, still others have an equally unhealthy belief that they are incredibly inadequate and have very little to offer in a conversation. They believe themselves to be losers with nothing worthy to offer. This too, is usually not the case and is a condition of low self-esteem typically found in those with a naturally quiet and subdued demeanor.

Give yourself a break. It's not all black and white. You don't know it all, nor should you and you certainly have plenty to offer if you only allow yourself to see that. You don't have to be an arrogant know-it-all bore or a meek little mouse. Confidence is sexy to point but can be obnoxious if overdone and people generally don't want to surround themselves with people who have absolutely nothing to say! You need to develop a middle ground.

In order to become interesting, become interested!

On a personal level, the secret for having more people want to engage in conversations with you is quite simple. Ask them questions! Almost everybody likes to talk about themself. The subject matter almost doesn't matter but obvious topics to ask about could include jobs, family, homes, pets, hobbies, etc. You may be thinking to yourself that you just really don't care about these people's personal lives. I was very much the same way for most of my life and the result of that, not surprisingly, was that I didn't have too many friends to speak of. What you will find is that by engaging in these types of conversations over and over, that you will begin to actually care and be interested in other people's lives. The tremendous benefit is that they will then, in turn, actually care about yours. Not only that, the whole back and forth dialog will be real and not forced. Again, the quality of these interactions will only be as rewarding and interesting as the extent to which you truly care and are invested. I found that one of the most useful things to do when interacting with others is to be honest about your feelings and knowledge regarding any particular subject. If somebody tells you that their hobby is stamp collecting and you know nothing about it, then say something like; "Oh, cool, I don't know anything about stamps, how did you get into that? Where do you find them? Do you belong to some kind of trading club, etc...?"

Read, learn, cultivate

It is completely natural to feel a bit intimidated, especially in a group setting, if people are talking about something that you know absolutely nothing about. Being "out of the loop" is an uncomfortable feeling. The best remedy for that is to know a little about a lot. Watch the news, read the paper and just observe what is going on around you. Again, when in doubt, ask!

Another equally important way to make yourself more interesting to those around you is to cultivate your own interests and hobbies. When you are passionate about something, your enthusiasm shows and is therefore interesting to others.

Be willing to transcend beyond your selfish instincts

Finally, you have to be willing to rise above ego-driven and selfish desires. Human nature is self-serving. Sometimes when we do nice things for others, the motivation to do so is to benefit ourselves by boosting our ego and feelings of importance. Be willing to ascribe to something higher than self-gratification.

By seeking the truth about yourself, you can transcend your own selfish nature and find contentment. If you are hurting yourself with drugs and booze, then you are not in harmony with those around you and are actually causing them harm. By doing the right thing for others and the world at large, you have the potential to find true enlightenment.

Drinking and drugging goes against your inner voice and deep down you know it. Besides free will, the greatest gift given to us by the universe is that of intuition. It will rarely let you down and it is a large part of the subject matter that will conclude our journey of self-discovery.

Chapter 19

Intuition, spirituality and beyond

I have no doubt that everything in this book up until now can benefit you if you are trying to overcome your alcoholism. This chapter deals with my personal feelings on intuition and spirituality in general. By no means do you need to agree with any of it in order to get sober and live a happier and more productive life. I simply offer it as it has great meaning to me and perhaps some of it will strike something within you.

I believe in intuition and that we should follow ours whenever possible. Let me share a story of my youth which is just one of many instances where I believe my intuition or "inner voice" was communicating with me.

The brook

When I was a young boy, about five years old, my family lived in a town that was separated by a cute little stream that ran right through the middle of it. We lived on a short dead end that ended right by the edge of the water. The kids who lived there generally hung out with those from "their" side of the brook. One day my older brother Tom, who was four years my senior, was gracious enough to let me tag along with his buddies for some fun down by the water. When we got there, there was a group of kids on the other side who challenged us to some kind of war-like game. I'm not even sure about what the rules were or what the game exactly was because I, as a little five year old, single handedly ended it before it even really got started. The way the game worked, the leader of either side could stop the action with a verbal command and everybody on each side had to freeze in place. Not understanding the rules and the fact that I was in my own little world anyway, I got bored and picked up a huge branch and just starting swinging it around and around in huge looping circles. Being that the branch was too big for my small hands, after half dozen or so rotations, it flew out of my hand and went airborne. As fate would have it, it sailed in what at the time seemed like slow motion and connected squarely into the head of the enemy's leader. The boy dropped like a ton of bricks and lay motionless. It was like time simply stopped. All of a sudden, everybody from my "team" simultaneously turned and ran for their lives.

I remember looking back before we exited the side of the brook to the street that we lived on and being just sick to my stomach. In what seemed like a split second, I felt fear, guilt and sincere sorrow for what I had done. I hoped with all my heart that that boy was OK. I couldn't understand why everybody else didn't feel the same way. We ran into our backyard and my brother and his friends were celebrating for God's sake! I just couldn't and didn't want to get it. My brother tried to raise me on his shoulders as some kind of Davey who just slayed Goliath. I pushed him away and ran into the garage and started wailing like a little baby. I sat in the corner in a little ball for what seemed like hours.

There was no reason for me not to follow the "herd" mentality and celebrate. But I simply couldn't. Something on an intuitive level told me that what had happened (hurting another human being) and what was happening now (the masses celebrating their "victory "at the expense of another's suffering), was just WRONG.

I was only five years old and had really never been taught that what I had done was wrong. I mean I was this little kid that practically never ventured from his backyard and didn't know anything about anything. My days were filled with playing with my Hot Wheels and plastic dinosaurs. The feeling of wrongness came from within. I didn't go through some kind of rational mental thought process to feel the way I did, I just did. My intuition told me so!

The "win at all costs" mentality is one that is taught from an early age. Granted its original basis is the result of our instinctual nature to overcome danger. However, as evolved beings, we should be able to rise above our ancestral caveman needs for power and domination. The tribal "us vs. them" mentality is pounded into us from day one. The mindset of our town, country, religion, etc., is better than yours, goes on and on! It never stops. Well, it pretty much did for me that day. I was never comfortable in that mindset. Sure I still like to compete and win, but I realize that it's just a game! I'm not going to try and kill my opponent! The other kids that I was with that day were all at least 4 years older than I was and had already been taught that this was the way of the world. Some of them of may have felt it was wrong but they went along with the crowd and celebrated anyway, even though their inner voice knew it was wrong.

I sincerely believe that intuition is our communication link with our subconscious or soul if you will. How else can you explain that "feeling" you get when you just know what to do in a situation, without any particular reason. Or how about that absolute conviction that something is right or wrong, without knowing all the facts.

So, I believe that intuition is very real and that it guides us to be who we are meant to be. If we ignore it, we are bound to have internal and conflicting thoughts and feelings.

That's why alcoholics and addicts alike are in such emotional turmoil. We know, on an intuitive level that what we are doing is wrong and not what we were meant for. If you live your life in alignment with that inner voice, you are far more likely to know peace and contentment.

Intuition- The arbitrator's best friend

Back in chapter 15, I discussed the struggle that we all have with the competing thoughts that race through our heads. I suggested various ways in which to empower the arbitrator within us. Again, he or she is the one who has the ultimate say in which voices are going to win the debate as to how proceed in our lives. If you utilize all of the ideas that I outlined, that by itself would be enough to help you master the internal dialog in your head. If, however, you do believe that intuition is real and that it is ultimately there to help you be true to yourself, then there is no more powerful tool at your disposal. After you've exhausted all of the other methods to help you make sound decisions, ask yourself if your final one rings true in your gut. Does it feel right? That my friend, is your intuition talking and it will rarely let you down.

Intuition often goes against what we or society wants us to do so we tend to dismiss it and take the easy path. Using alcohol or drugs is a prime example of that. On a deep level, you know that what you are doing is not right. But we do it anyway. That's how strong the addictive monster is. If you listen to your heart, believe it, and act on what it is trying to tell you, the monster doesn't have a chance.

Spirituality versus organized religion

Take your pick of religions, prophets, and Holy Scriptures. They are all, every last one of them, an advocate of the "golden rule" and ideals such as thou shalt not kill, etc...

The problem is that almost all religions have this warped belief that their God, and their message, is the only one with any merit. It is pervasive to the point that they teach that only those who "believe" as they do, have any hope of reaching a peaceful afterlife in heaven or wherever.

Let me ask you this. If God, the universe, the guiding force, or however you want to label it, is all loving and altruistic, would that same entity seriously consider banishing those who did not believe in a particular way to an eternity in less favorable conditions than those who did? What does your gut or intuition tell you about that take? If you are truly honest with yourself and listen to your inner voice, I think you know the answer to that.

I believe that the great prophets and sages of history, wherever they may be or in whatever form they exist, if in fact they do exist in some way, are screaming and crying at the same time over the amount of blood that has been spilled over the centuries over which group has it right.

I also think that the great thinkers and religious leaders did in fact, for the most part, have it right. It's just that over the centuries their messages have been diluted. The insatiable need of the leaders of certain ideologies to be right, and to force others to see it their way, has caused unthinkable suffering to the point of madness.

The original prophets and saints were all spiritual teachers and didn't seek to start organized religions. That was taken care of by their "well intentioned" faithful followers.

I am by no means trying to insinuate that organized religions are bad. Like AA, I think you need to take and nurture what is good about the "message" and the institution and leave the rest.

You are a spiritual creature. If you follow your heart, are good to your fellow man and do the next right thing because you are moved to do so, then there will be no heaviness in your soul and addiction will have no hold on you.

Conclusion

While this whole book leans heavily on the fact that the decision to get well is yours and yours alone, I don't want to give off the false impression that I am advocating being an island in the sea of recovery and life. As previously stated, most alcoholics and addicts slowly and progressively isolate themselves from their family, friends, co-workers and the world at large and think that they somehow can do life on their own. In order to regain sound mental health, one has to rediscover an interest in those around them. The notion that you will get well and then re-join the human race in order to give of yourself and help your fellow man is indeed extremely altruistic, right and noble. It is a huge step but in and of itself, it is still not enough.

The paradox lies in the fact that in order to be a giving and empathetic soul, you also have to accept and value the help, caring and guidance from others regarding yourself. If you don't, then there is a better than average chance that all of your efforts of "making a difference" are really just some form of ego gratification. It is essential that you allow yourself to risk the vulnerability and possible hurt that is an inevitable possibility that comes with letting others into your heart and mind. It is in this "give and take" way of interacting with the world by which we are truly able to find peace and a sense of community.

Not the end but a new beginning

Well dear reader, we have almost reached the end of what I hope has been a discussion that offers some real constructive information that YOU can utilize to determine YOUR destiny.

By the time most people even entertain the idea of picking up a book which addresses their drinking dilemma, they have moved beyond the denial phase and are at least willing to take an inward look at themselves to see what, if anything, should be done about it. Here are just a few of the conclusions that you might come up with as to what course of action that you should take;

1-You can decide not to decide and remain in your dark hole and be miserable. As I've mentioned before, deciding not to take any action is still a choice and not a very good one. The fact that you are here would be a pretty clear indication that you've come to the conclusion that there has to be a better way.

2-You can enlist the help of therapists, 30 day rehabilitation programs, hospital in-patient or out-patient services, licensed drug and alcohol counselors, etc. While any of these methods are clearly better than doing nothing, their success rate is minimal at best.

3-You can choose the AA way and turn your life and free will over to God, some other higher power or the AA group itself. It may keep you sober but at the cost of giving up being a self-determining person who creates his or her own reality and destiny. This way of living demands that you accept without question the guidance provided. In organized religion the word of God is handed down via your church, pastor or priest and the written word of Holy Scripture (Bible, Koran, etc.). In AA it is the word of their founding prophet, Bill Wilson, found in the "Big Book" and in the 12 steps preached at AA meetings around the world. Like many organized religions, AA instructs that if you leave the flock that you will surely be condemned to a life without salvation. In other words, you will drink alcoholically again. This is a lie. As I have discussed, AA can certainly be of great benefit to you at the beginning of your recovery but it should not become a way of life. It locks you into reliving your past with labels, guilt and dependence.

4-Finally, you can choose to chart your own path and fulfill your limitless human potential. More people achieve sobriety every day on their own than they do with any other method previously listed. Sobriety and living well is a choice and it is yours and yours alone to make.

My dear old dad used to tell me to just drink in moderation. You know, have two or three and then just stop for the night. He sooo didn't get it. You and I both know that it just doesn't work that way for us. It's all or nothing.

So is it as simple as just saying no? Well, yes and no. Ultimately it's not that complicated and that's exactly what you have to do. Is it easy? Hell no. Like so many things in life, it's a decision.

You can do it if you DECIDE to do it!

For this decision to have any real chance at succeeding, there are several elements that need to be present, realities that you must embrace and things that you must do;

1-*Desire*- You have to truly want this for YOURSELF. You can't do it because you want to appease your spouse, children, boss, etc... You have to want it more than anything else because your life depends on it.

2-*Knowledge*- They say that knowledge is power, which further emphasizes my whole premise that you are not powerless. In order to evolve and grow you have to be a life-long learner. Hopefully this book will be a good start in learning better thinking, listening, and decision making skills but by no means should you consider your education as finished. There is so much out there in other books, the internet and from those who have already traveled this path. You want to get well and change your life for the better so you need to learn new ways of living and interacting with the world that you live in.

3-*Forgiveness*- Give yourself a break and forgive yourself for having developed this condition. You didn't do it on purpose! You simply lost your way. Some of us have endured horrific tragedies and living conditions. That is all the more reason to cut yourself some slack. Even if your addiction was completely self-inflicted for no particular reason, it doesn't matter. That part of your life can be history if you choose to make it so. The beautiful thing about life and free will is that you always get a do over. Start now.

4-*Belief*- Sincerely believe that life is better sober because it really is. At the time of this writing I will have entered the third year of my sober re-birth. It's not even a little bit of stretch to state that it has been the best period of my life. Most importantly, believe that you deserve it because you do!

5-*Action*- All the best intentions and dreams will go unfulfilled unless you take action now. If not now, then when?

6-*Gratitude*- Don't ever take your sobriety for granted. You are giving yourself a second chance at life. It is hard work and very easy to undo. You may slip and fall along the way and that's OK. Just dust yourself off and start anew. Be thankful that you are still here and have the opportunity to embark on a new life that can be better than you have ever imagined.

7-*Pride*- What you are doing is a truly courageous act. It takes guts, determination, extremely hard work and patience. To Hell with being humble about it; scream out to the world that you have re-entered society and are damned proud of what you have accomplished!

8-*Acceptance and change*- Pretty much what this whole book is about.

9-*Noble intent and selflessness*- It's not all about you. See Chapter 18.

10-*Presence*-It's a recurring theme throughout the book but it gets one final nod here. **Life is now!** So much of AA is supposedly about living in the present by living "one day at a time". The paradox is that so much of AA protocol achieves the exact opposite. The AA way involves constantly talking about and reliving your alcoholic, "sinful" past, introducing yourself as an alcoholic and telling your story over and over again.

11-*Self-determination as opposed to pre-determination*-If you turn your will over to "something" else then it logically follows that you are not responsible for, or have any determination over what occurs in your life. God's will be done. If that's your belief, then you don't have to "think" or "stress" about anything past, present or future. If all is pre-determined, then life is just a carefree movie; what fun! If you believe that the events of your life are predestined and are going to happen regardless of what you do to influence it, then AA might very well be an excellent place to set up camp. Why not? It will give you a set of "suggestions" (steps) to live by and leaders to tell you what to do. If you don't believe that your ability to make decisions matters, then let AA and your higher power make them for you. If, however, you believe that you can and should control your own destiny to the best of your ability, then that power is available to you.

So what's wrong with having a Higher Power?

Absolutely nothing! The thing is that you don't have to have one to become sober. The only way that would hold true is if you embrace AA's major premise that you are powerless to change on your own accord. If you don't buy that notion, then you don't need to hand your life over to God, AA, or any other "higher power" to get well.

The well renowned German philosopher, Friedrich Nietzsche, boldly stated that 'God is dead'. Don't get crazy on me, I believe in God, a higher power, universal intelligence or something. What he meant by that statement is that mankind long ago chose to forge his own path. Take the "story" of Adam and Eve for example. When Adam ate the apple, he decided to determine his own future. He chose free will! That's what the universe wants us to do. Whether you like it or not, the gift of free will is ours to embrace or ignore. If you embrace it, life will become much more challenging but at the same time, infinitely more interesting and rewarding if you choose well.

I'll say it one last time; sobriety is a choice and the choice is yours! So decide to decide and be the author and shaper of your life.

You are not POWERLESS! Evolve, recover and set yourself free. I did it and so can you!

Peace,

Rolf

Notes

Chapter 2

Elizabeth Kubler-Ross, *On Death and Dying*, (New York, NY: The MacMillan Company, 1969)

Chapter 3

Alcoholics Anonymous World Services, Inc., *Alcoholics Anonymous, 4th addition,* (Alcoholics Anonymous World Services, Inc., 2001), page 58

Chapter 4

The layman with a notebook; With a forward by L.W. Grensted, *What is the Oxford Group?*, (Oxford University Press, 1933), pages 8-9

William James, *The Varieties of Religious Experience*, (Modern Library, 1936), page 525

Alcoholics Anonymous World Services, Inc., *Twelve Steps and Twelve Traditions, 63rd printing,* (Alcoholics Anonymous World Services, Inc., 2002), pages 26, 27, 36, 37, 30

Alcoholics Anonymous, pages 44-45, 49, 52-53, 45, 45

Chapter 6

Twelve Steps and Twelve Traditions, pages 43, 44, 50, 50, 56, 56

Alcoholics Anonymous, pages 66, 64, 69, 70

Chapter 7

Twelve Steps and Twelve Traditions, pages 63, 63, 70, 72

Dictionary.com. humility. Retrieved September 20, 2012 from http://dictionary.reference.com/browse/humble

Dictionary.com. humble. Retrieved September 20, 2012 from http://dictionary.reference.com/browse/humble?s=t

Wikipedia. Humility. Retrieved September 20, 2012 from http://en.wikipedia.org/wiki/Humility

Chapter 9

Alcoholics Anonymous, pages 58, 60, 83-84

AA Preamble-Copyright by the AA Grapevine, Inc.

Bibliography

Alcoholics Anonymous World Services, *Alcoholics Anonymous, 4th addition,* (New York, NY: Alcoholics Anonymous World Services, Inc., 2001)

Alcoholics Anonymous World Services, *Pass It On: The Story of Bill Wilson and How the A.A. Message Reached the World,* (New York, NY: Alcoholics Anonymous World Services, 1984)

Alcoholics Anonymous World Services, *Twelve Steps and Twelve Traditions, 63rd printing,* (Alcoholics Anonymous World Services, Inc., 2002)

Cheever, Susan, *My Name Is Bill: Bill Wilson--His Life and the Creation of Alcoholics Anonymous,* (New York, NY: Simon & Schuster, 2004)

Gregson, David and Jay S. Efran, Ph.D, *The Tao of Sobriety,* (New York, NY: St. Martin's Press, 2002)

Hartigan, Francis, *Bill W.: A Biography of Alcoholics Anonymous Cofounder Bill Wilson,* (New York, NY: St. Martin's Press, 2000)

James, William, *The Varieties of Religious Experience,* (Modern Library, 1936)

Panza, Christopher, PhD and Gregory Gale, MA, *Existentialism for Dummies,* (Indianapolis, IN: Wiley Publishing, Inc.)

Peck, M. Scott, MD, *The Road Less Traveled and Beyond,* (New York, NY: Touchstone, 1997)

Tolle, Eckhart, *The Power of Now,* (Novato, CA: New World Library, 1999)

Vaughn, Clark, *Addictive drinking: the road to recovery for problem drinkers and those who love them, (NY, NY: Viking Press, 1982)*

Wade, Nicholas, *The Faith Instinct: How Religion Evolved and Why It Endures,* (The Penguin Press, 2009)

26816428R00098

Made in the USA
Lexington, KY
16 October 2013